HIDDEN TREASURE REVEALED

Memorizing God's Word

with

BIBLE STUDY ANSWERS

Using the King James Version

Compiled by Nancy Dunnewin

TEACH Services, Inc.
PUBLISHING
www.TEACHServices.com • (800) 367-1844

ISBN-13: 978-1-4796-1441-7 (Paperback)
ISBN-13: 978-1-4796-1530-8 (Spiral)
ISBN-13: 978-1-4796-1442-4 (ePub)
Library of Congress Control Number: 2022906781

Published by

TEACH Services, Inc.
P U B L I S H I N G
www.TEACHServices.com • (800) 367-1844

TABLE OF CONTENTS

BIBLE STUDY TOPIC

Praise for *Hidden Treasure Revealed with Bible Study Answers…*

"In a world of distractions, this is a refreshing call back to the basics. Twenty-five essential topics presented concisely from the Bible itself, with tips for Bible marking and memorization. What a great tool!"

—Ken LeBrun,
Pastor

"Nancy Dunnewin's latest book from TEACH Services is the perfect resource for preparing Bible studies, engaging in Bible memorization, or marking out a topical chain reference in your own Bible. Dunnewin includes major topics of interest for Seventh-day Adventists who are anxiously awaiting 'that day' (1 Thess 5:4)."

—Stephen Reasor,
Associate Professor of Religious Studies, Burman University

"Refreshing clarity and simplicity—Bible topics in *Hidden Treasure Revealed with Bible Study Answers* are put together in a way that offers insight and inspires the desire to study more. It is also an excellent tool to use for personal or group Bible memorization. Thank you, Nancy, for your dedication in compiling a valuable study book for Bible students of all ages. 'THY WORD IS A LAMP UNTO MY FEET, AND A LIGHT UNTO MY PATH' (Ps. 119:105)."

—Pat Marsh,
Retired RN, Washington

"*Hidden Treasure Revealed* gives you all the tools you need for effectively storing your mind with Bible treasures of inestimable value. I highly recommend this method of memorization for young or old. I have used it for many years. And now I have it with my favorite Bible studies!"

—Lisa Quade,
Feeding His Lambs Ministries

	BIBLE STUDY TOPIC	CODES	1st BIBLE TEXT
1	Inspiration of the Bible	IB	John 14:6
2	Origin of Sin	OS	I John 3:8
3	Salvation	SA	Acts 16:30
4	Heaven and New Earth	NE	John 14:1–3
5	God's Law	GL	Exodus 31:18
6	God's Sabbath	GS	Genesis 2:1–3
7	How to Keep the Sabbath	KS	Exodus 20:8
8	First Day, The	FD	Matthew 28:1
9	Signs of His Coming	HC	Matthew 24:3–8
10	Second Coming, The	SC	John 14:1–3
11	Baptism	BP	Mark 16:16
12	Spirit of Prophecy, The	SP	Revelation 12:17
13	Healthful Living	HL	Genesis 1:29
14	Stewardship	SS	Matthew 6:31–33
15	Sanctuary, The	TS	Exodus 25:8
16	Judgement, The	JM	Acts 17:30–31
17	Church Standards	CS	Philippians 4:8
18	State of the Dead	SD	Genesis 2:17
19	Millennium, The	ML	Revelation 6:14–17
20	Little Horn, The	LH	Daniel 7:4–7
21	Mark of the Beast	MB	Exodus 20:8–11
22	Three Angels' Messages	TA	Revelation 14:6–7
23	Seven Last Plagues	LP	Revelation 16:1–2
24	Trust and Obey	TO	Psalm 139:23–24
25	True Church, The	TC	Jeremiah 6:2

HIDDEN TREASURE

Memorizing God's Word

This book of Bible studies is designed to encourage you to memorize God's Word. Commit His Word into your heart so that you may be able to withstand the temptations of the devil (Ephesians 6:11), to speak a word in season to him that is in need (Isaiah 50:4), and to be able to give a reason for your faith (I Peter 3:15).

Take God's Word and study it, memorize it, as if looking for hidden treasure. Those who do this will receive a blessing that only God can give. Truth will be revealed to you that will change your life forever.

These Bible studies with their Bible answers use the first two words and the first letter of the subsequent words, which helps to memorize God's Word. The complete Bible study answers are at the end of this book.

These Bible studies may also be used to mark your Bible, using the two-letter code from each topic. For example, find John 14:6 from number one in lesson 1 and highlight the text in your Bible; then write John 17:17 IB near the highlighted text. Next, highlight John 17:17 and write II Tim. 3:15–17 IB, and so on.

May God bless you richly as you study and memorize His Word, searching as you would for hidden treasure.

1

INSPIRATION OF THE BIBLE—IB

1. What did Jesus say about Himself? John 14:6
2. What is truth? John 17:17
3. Is scripture inspired? II Timothy 3:15–17
4. Where did scripture come from? II Peter 1:21
5. Why was the Old Testament (OT) written? Romans 15:4
6. Did Jesus use the OT? Luke 24:27
7. What should man live by? Matthew 4:4
8. What can the words of Jesus do? John 6:63
9. What should we do with God's Word? Psalm 119:11
10. What is God's Word to us? Psalm 119:105

1—IB

1. John 14:6	Jesus saith u h, I a t w, t t, a t l; n m c u t F, b b M.
2. John 17:17	Sanctify them t T t, T w i t.
3. II Timothy 3:15–17	And that f a c t h k t h S, w a a t m t w u s t f w i i C J. A S i g b i o G, a i p f d, f r, f c, f i i r: T t m o G m b p, t f u a g w.
4. II Peter 1:21	For the p c n i o t b t w o m, b h m o G s a t w m b t H G.
5. Romans 15:4	For whatsoever t w w a w w f o l, t w t p a c o t S m h h.
6. Luke 24:27	And beginning a M a a t p, H e u t i a t S t t c H.
7. Matthew 4:4	But He a a s, I i w, m s n l b b a, b b e w t p o o t m o G.
8. John 6:63	It is t S t q; t f p n: t w t I s u y, t a s, a t a l.
9. Psalm 119:11	Thy word h I h i m h t I m n s a T.
10. Psalm 119:105	Thy word i a l u m f a a l u m p.

2

ORIGIN OF SIN—OS

1. Where did sin originate? I John 3:8
2. Who was Lucifer? Ezekiel 28:14–15
3. Who did Lucifer want to be like? Isaiah 14:12–14
4. What happened to Lucifer in heaven? Revelation 12:7–9
5. Should we be concerned? Revelation 12:12
6. How is Satan behaving now? I Peter 5:8
7. What warning did God give Adam and Eve? Genesis 2:17
8. What lie did Satan tell Eve? Genesis 3:1–4
9. What is sin? I John 3:4
10. How many have sinned? Romans 3:23
11. Is there hope? Romans 3:24; John 3:16
12. Will sin and affliction rise again? Nahum 1:9

2—OS

1. 1 John 3:8	He that c s i o t d; f t d s f t b.
2. Ezekiel 28:14–15	Thou art t a c t c; a I h s t s: t w u t h m o G...T w p i t w f t d t t w c, t i w f i t.
3. Isaiah 14:12–14	How art t f f h, O L, s o t m! h a t c d t t g, w d w t n! F t h s i t h, I w a i h, I w e m t a t s o G... I w b l t m H.
4. Revelation 12:7–9	And there w w i h: M a H a f a t d; a t d f a h a, A p n; n w t p f a m i h. A t g d w c o, t o s, c t D, a S, w d t w w: h w c o i t e, a h a w c o w h.
5. Revelation 12:12	Woe to t i o t e a o t s! f t d i c d u y, h g w, b h k t h h b a s t.
6. 1 Peter 5:8	Be sober, b v; b y a t d, a a r l, w a s w h m d.
7. Genesis 2:17	But of t t o t k o g a e, t s n e o i: f i t d t t e t t s s d.
8. Genesis 3:1–4	Now the s w m s t a b o t f w t L G h m. A h s u t w, Y, h G s, Y s n e o e t o t g? A t w s u t s, W m e o t f o t t o t g; B o t f o t t w i i t m o t g, G h s, Y s n e o i, n s y t i, l y d. A t s s u t w, Y s n s d.
9. I John 3:4	Whosoever committeth s t a t l: f s i t t o t l.
10. Romans 3:23	For all h s, a c s o t g o G.
11. Romans 3:24	Being justified f b H g t t r t i i C J.
11b. John 3:16	F G s l t w, t H g H o b S, t w b i H s n p, b h e l.
12. Nahum 1:9	What do y i a t L? H w m a u e: a s n r u t s t.

3

SALVATION—SA

1. What Question did the jailer ask? Acts 16:30
2. What must we do to be saved? Acts 16:31; Mark 16:16
3. What are the wages of sin and the gift of God? Romans 6:23
4. How do we know God loves us? Romans 5:8
5. How do we become justified? Romans 3:23–24
6. What did God do for us? I John 4:9–11
7. Why did He do it? John 3:16
8. How is a man born again? John 3:3–5
9. What happens when we confess our sins? I John 1:9
10. Can man change? II Corinthians 5:17 (see also Romans 6:6)
11. What else will God do for us? John 1:12
12. What is Jesus' plea to you and me today? Revelation 3:20

3—SA

1. Acts 16:30	And brought t o, a s, S, w m I d t b s?
2. Acts 16:31	And they s, B o t L J C, a t s b s, a t h.
2b. Mark 16:16	He that b a i b s b s; b h t b n s b d.
3. Romans 6:23	For the w o s i d; b t g o G i e l t J C o L.
4. Romans 5:8	But God c H l t u, i t, w w w y s, C d f u.
5. Romans 3:23–24	For all h s, a c s o t g o G. B j f b H g t t r t i i C J.
6. I John 4:9–11	In this w m t l o G t u, b t G s h o b S i t w, t w m l t H. H i l, n t w l G, b t H l u, a s H S t b t p f o s. B, i G s l u, w o a t l o a.
7. John 3:16	For God s l t w, t H g H o b S, t w b i H s n p, b h e l.
8. John 3:3–5	Jesus answered a s u h, V, v, I s u t, E a m b b a, h c s t k o G. N s u h, H c a m b b w h i o? C h e t s t i h m w a b b? J a, V, v, I s u t, E a m b b o w a o t S, h c e i t k o G.
9. I John 1:9	If we c o s, H i f a j t f u o s, a t c u f a u.
10. II Corinthians 5:17	Therefore if a m b i C, h i a n c: o t a p a; b, a t a b n. (see also Rom. 6:6)
11. John 1:12	But as m a r H, t t g H p t b t s o G, e t t t b o H n.
12. Revelation 3:20	Behold, I s a t d, a k: i a m h m v, a o t d, I w c i t h, a w s w h, a h w M.

4

HEAVEN and NEW EARTH—NE

1. Is there a heaven? John 14:1–3
2. What did Abraham look for? Hebrews 11:10
3. Who knows what God has prepared for us? I Corinthians 2:9
4. What did John the Revelator see? Revelation 21:1–4
5. Describe the Holy City. Revelation 21:10–11, 21
6. What else has God prepared? Revelation 22:1–2
7. Will we ever have to be afraid there? Isaiah 11:6–9
8. What will we do in the New Earth? Isaiah 65:21–22
9. Will anyone ever get sick? Isaiah 33:24
10. Will we recognize our loved ones? I Corinthians 13:12
11. Who will have the right to all of this? Revelation 22:14

4—NE

1. John 14:1–3	Let not y h b t: y b i G, b a i M. I M F h a m m: i i w n s, I w h t y. I g t p a p f y. A i I g a p a p f y, I w c a, a r y u M; t w I a, t y m b a.
2. Hebrews 11:10	For he l f a c w h f w b a m i G.
3. I Corinthians 2:9	But as i i w, E h n s, n e h, n h e i t h o m, t t w G h p f t t l H.
4. Revelation 21:1–4	And I s a n h a a n e: f t f h a t f e w p a; at w n m s. A I J s t h c, n J, c d f G o o h, p a a b a f h h. A I h a g v o o h s, B, t t o G i w m, a h w d w t, a t s b h p, a G H s b w t, a b t G. A G s w a a t f t e; a t s b n m d, n s, n c, n s t b a m p: f t f t a p a.
5. Revelation 21:10–11, 21	And He c m a i t s t a g a h m, a s m t g c, t h J, d o o h f G, H t g o G: a h l w l u a s m p, e l a j s, c a c;... A t t g w t p: e s g w o o p: a t s o t c w p g, a i w t g.
6. Revelation 22:1–2	And he s m a p r o w o l, c a c, p o o t t o G a o t L. I t m o t s o i, a o e s o t r, w t t t o l, w b t m o f, a y h f e m: a t l o t t w f t h o t n.
7. Isaiah 11:6–9	The wolf a s d w t l, a t l s l d w t k; a t c a t y l a t f t; a a l c s l t. A t c a t b s f; t y o s l d t: a t l s e s l t o. A t s c s p o t h o t a, a t w c s p h h o t c d. T s n h n d i a m h m: f t e s b f o t k o t L, a t w c t s.
8. Isaiah 65:21–22	And they s b h, a i t, a t s p v, a e t f o t. T s n b, a a i; t s n p, a a e: f a t d o a t a t d o m p, a m e s l e t w o t h.
9. Isaiah 33:24	And the i s n s, I a s: t p t d t s b f t i.
10. I Corinthians 13:12	For now w s t a g, d; b t f t f: n I k i p; b t s I k e a a I a k.
11. Revelation 22:14	Blessed are t t d H c, t t m h r t t t o l, a m e i t t g i t c.

5

GOD'S LAW—GL

1. Where did Moses get the Ten Commandments and who wrote them? Exodus 31:18
2. How do we know if we sin? Romans 3:20
3. Without law what would we be unaware of? Romans 4:15
4. What is sin? I John 3:4
5. What is man's responsibility to God? Ecclesiastes 12:13
6. How long will God's law endure? Psalm 111:7–8
7. Is God's law good? Romans 7:12
8. Did Jesus change the law? Matthew 5:17–19
9. How many commandments are found in the New Testament (NT)? Matthew 22:36–40
10. Can we throw away any part of the Bible? James 2:10
11. How do we know if we love God? I John 5:1–3
12. How does God know we love Him? I John 2:3–6; John 14:15
13. How permanent is God's law? Luke 16:17

5—GL

1. Exodus 31:18	And He g u M, w H h m a e o c w h u M S, t t o t, t o s, w w t f o G.
2. Romans 3:20	Therefore by t d o t l t s n f b j i H s: f b t l i t k o s.
3. Romans 4:15	Because the l w w: f w n l i, t i n t.
4. I John 3:4	Whosoever committeth s t a t l: f s i t t o t l.
5. Ecclesiastes 12:13	Let us h t c o t w m: F G, a k H c: f t i t w d o m.
6. Psalm 111:7–8	The works o H h a v a j; a H c a s. T s f f e a e, a a d i t a u.
7. Romans 7:12	Wherefore the l i h, a t c h, a j, a g.
8. Matthew 5:17–19	Think not t I a c t d t l, o t p: I a n c t d, b t f. F v I s u y, t h a e p, o j o o t s i n w p f t l, t a b f. W t s b o o t l c, a s t m s, h s b c t l i t k o h: b w s d a t t, t s s b c g i t k o h.
9. Matthew 22:36–40	Master, which i t g c i t l? J s u h, T s l t L t G w a t h, a w a t s, a w a t m. T i t f a g c. A t s i l u i, T s l t n a t. O t t c h a t l a t p.
10. James 2:10	For whosoever s k t w l, a y o i o p, h i g o a.
11. I John 5:1–3	Whosoever believeth, t J i t C i b o G: a e o t l H t b l H a t i b o H. B t w k t w l t c o G, w w l G, a k H c. F t i t l o G, t w k H c: a H c a n g.
12. I John 2:3–6	And hereby w d k t w k H, i w k H c. H t s, I k H, a k n H c, i a l, a t t i n i h. B w k H w, i h v i t l o G p: h k w t w a i H. H t s h a i H o h a s t w, e a H w.
12b. John 14:15	If ye l m, k m c.
13. Luke 16:17	And it i e f h a e t p, t o t o t l t f.

6

GOD'S SABBATH—GS

1. What did God do after creating the world? Genesis 2:1–3
2. Did God mention the Sabbath in His Commandments.? Exodus 20:8–11
3. Of what is the Sabbath a sign? Ezekiel 20:12, 20
4. On what day did Jesus worship? Luke 4:16
5. On what day did Paul worship? Acts 17:2
6. What day of the week did Jesus' followers keep holy? Luke 23:56
7. Will Sabbath be kept in heaven? Isaiah 66:22–23
8. Who was the Sabbath made for? Mark 2:27–28
9. What blessing comes to those who keep Sabbath? Isaiah 58:13–14
10. Does it matter what day we keep? James 2:10

6—GS

1. Genesis 2:1–3	Thus the h a t e w f, a a t h o t. A o t s d G e H w w H h m; a H r o t s d f a H w w H h m. A G b t s d, a s i: b t i i H h r f a H w w G c a m.
2. Exodus 20:8–11	Remember the s d, t k i h. S d s t l, a d a t w: B t s d i t S o t L t G: i i t s n d a w, t, n t s, n t d, t m, n t m, n t c, n t s t i w t g: F i s d t L m h a e, t s, a a t i t i, a r t s d: w t L b t S d, a h i.
3. Ezekiel 20:12, 20	Moreover also I g t m S, t b a s b M a t, t t m k t I a t L t s t.... A h m S; a t s b a s b m a y, t y m k t I a t L y G.
4. Luke 4:16	And He c t N, w H h b b u: a, a H c w, H w i t s o t S d, a s u f t r.
5. Acts 17:2	And Paul, a h m w, w i u t, a t S d r w t o o t S.
6. Luke 23:56	And they r, a p s a o; a r t S d a t t c.
7. Isaiah 66:22–23	For as t n h a t n e, w I w m, s r b m, s t L, s s y s a y n r. A i s c t p, t f o n m t a, a f o S t a, s a f c t w b m, s t L.
8. Mark 2:27–28	And He s u t, T S w m f m, a n m f t S: T t S o m i L a o t S.
9. Isaiah 58:13–14	If thou t a t f f t S, f d t p o m h d; a c t S a d, t h o t L, h; a s h H, n d t o w, n f t o p, n s t o w: T s t d t i t L; a I w c t t r u t h p o t e, a f t w t h o J t f: f t m o t L h s i.
10. James 2:10	For whosoever s k t w l, a y o i o p, h i g o a.

7

HOW TO KEEP THE SABBATH—KS

1. What did Jesus say about the Sabbath? Exodus 20:8
2. How long was each day of creation? Genesis 1:5, 13, 31
3. When does Sabbath begin and end? Leviticus 23:32
4. What is the preparation day? Mark 15:42
5. Is Sabbath observance important? Exodus 16:29–30
6. Why were the Jews condemned in Nehemiah's time? Nehemiah 13:16–18
7. How do we keep the Sabbath holy? Isaiah 58:12–14
8. Should we help others on Sabbath? Matthew 12:10–13
9. Why is Sabbath observance so important? Ezekiel 20:12, 20

7—KS

1. Exodus 20:8	Remember the S d, t k i h.
2. Genesis 1:5, 13, 31	...and the e a t m w t f d...a t e a t m w t t d...a t e a t m w t s d.
3. Leviticus 23:32	It shall b u y a s o r, a y s a y s: i t n d o t m a e, f e u e, s y c y s.
4. Mark 15:42	And now w t e w c, b i w t p, t i, t d b t S.
5. Exodus 16:29–30	See, for t L h g y t S, t H g y o t s d t b o t d; a y e m i h p, l n m g o o h p o t s d. S t p r o t s d.
6. Nehemiah 13:16–18	There dwelt m o T a t, w b f, a a m o w, a s o t S u t c o J, a i J. T I c w t n o J, a s u t, W e t i t t y d, a p t S d? D n y f t, a d n o G b a t e u u, a u t c? y y b m w u I b p t S.
7. Isaiah 58:12–14	And they t s b o t s b t o w p: t s r u t f o m g; a t s b c, T r o t b, T r o p t d i. I t t a t f f t S, f d t p o M h d; a c t S a d, t h o t L, h; a s h H, n d t o w, n f t o p, n s t o w: T s t d t i t L; a I w c t t r u t h p o t e, a f t w t h o J t f: f t m o t L h s i.
8. Matthew 12:10–13	And, behold, t w a m w h h h w. A t a H, s, I i l t h o t S d? t t m a H. A H s u t, W m s t b a y, t s h o s, a i i f i a p o t S d, w h n l h o i, a l i o? H m t i a m b t a s? W i i l t d w o t S d. T s H t t m, S f t h. A h s i f; a i w r w, l a t o.
9. Ezekiel 20:12, 20	Moreover also I g t M S, t b a s b M a t, t t m k t I a t L t s t....A h M S; a t s b a s b M a y, t y m k t I a t L y G.

8

THE FIRST DAY—FD

1. What does Matthew say about the first day? Matthew 28:1
2. What does Mark say? Mark 16:2, 9
3. Read Luke's account. Luke 24:1
4. Read John's account. John 20:1
5. What did God do on the first day of creation? Genesis 1:3–5
6. What did the disciples do after the crucifixion? John 20:19
7. Did the disciples take up offerings on the first day? I Corinthians 16:2
8. Didn't Paul preach for communion on the first day? Acts 20:7
9. What does it mean to break bread? Acts 2:46
10. Why do most people worship on Sunday? Matthew 15:9
11. What day is called the Lord's day? Revelation 1:10
12. Compare Mark 2:27–28 (See also Matthew 12:8)

8—FD

1. Matthew 28:1	In the e o t S, a i b t d t t f d o t w, c M M a t o M t s t s.
2. Mark 16:2, 9	And very e i t m t f d o t w, t c u t s a t r o t s.... Now when J w r e t f d o t w, H a f t M M, o o w H h c s d.
3. Luke 24:1	Now upon t f d o t w, v e i t m, t c u t s, b t s w t h p, a c o w t.
4. John 20:1	The first d o t w c M M e, w i w y d, u t s, a s t s t a f t s.
5. Genesis 1:3–5	And God s, L t b l: a t w l. A G s t l, t I w g: a G d t l f t d, A G c t l D, a t d H c N. A t e a t m w t f d.
6. John 20:19	Then the s d a e, b t f d o t w, w t d w s w t d w a f f o t J, c J a s i t m, a s u t, P b u y.
7. I Corinthians 16:2	Upon the f d o t w l e o o y l b h i s, a G h p h, t t b n g w I c.
8. Acts 20:7	And upon t f d o t w, w t d c t t b b, P p u t, r t d o t m; a c h s u m.
9. Acts 2:46	And they, c d w o a i t t, a b b f h t h, d e t m w g a s o h.
10. Matthew 15:9	But in v t d w M, t f d t c o m.
11. Revelation 1:10	I was i t S o t L d, a h b m a g v, a o a t.
12. Mark 2:27–28	And He s u t, t S w m f m, a n m f t S: T t S o m i L a o t S. (See also Matt. 12:8)

9

SIGNS OF HIS COMING—HC

1. What six signs did Jesus begin with? Matthew 24:3–8
2. What does Daniel say about the last days? Daniel 12:1, 4
3. Will everyone believe these signs? 2 Peter 3:3–5, 8–9
4. What will people be like in the last days? 2 Timothy 3:1–5
5. How will Satan deceive many? I Timothy 4:1–2
6. Will there be signs in our own galaxy? Matthew 24:29
7. Will there be a time of trouble? Matthew 24:19–27
8. What is the last prophecy to be fulfilled? Matthew 24:14
9. What will be the final event? Matthew 24:30

9—HC

1. Matthew 24:3–8	And as H s u t m o O, t d c u H p, s, T u, w s t t b? A w s b t s o T c, a o t e o t w? A J a a s u t, T h t n m d y. F m s c i m n, s, I a C; a s d m. A y s h o w a r o w: s t y b n t: f a t t m c t p, b t e i n y. F n s r a n, a k a k: a t s b f, a p, a e, i d p. A t a t b o s.
2. Daniel 12:1, 4	And at t t s M s u, t g p w s f t c o t p: a t s b a t o t, s a n w s t w a n e t t s t: a a t t t p s b d, e o t s b f w i t b....But thou, O D, s u t w, a s t b, e t t t o t e: m s r t a f, a k s b i.
3. II Peter 3:3–5, 8–9	Knowing this f, t t s c i t l d s, w a t o l, A s, W i t p o H c? F s t f f a, a t c a t w f t b o t c. F t t w a i o, t b t w o G t h w o o, a t e s o o t w a i t w... But, beloved, b n i o t o t, t o d i w t L a a t y, a a t y a o d. T L i n s c H p a s m c s; b i l t u-w, n w t a s p, b t a s c t r.
4. II Timothy 3:1–5	This know a, t i t l d p t s c. F m s b l o t o s, c, b, p, b, d t p, u , u, W n a, t, f a, i, f, d o t t a g, T, h, h, l o p m t l o G; H a f o g, b d t p t: f s t a.
5. I Timothy 4:1–2	Now the S s e, t i t l t s s d f t f, g h t s s, a d o d; S l i h; h t c s w a h i.
6. Matthew 24:29	Immediately after t t o t d s t s b d, a t m s n g h l, a t s s f f h, a t p o t h s b s.
7. Matthew 24:19–27	And woe u t t a w c, a t t t g s i t d! B p y t y f b n i t w, n o t S d; F t s b g t, s a w n s t b o t w t t t, n, n e s b. A e t d s b s, t s n f b s: b f t e s t d s b s. T i a m s s u y, L, h i C, o t; b i n. F t s a f C, a f p, a s s g s a w; i t, i i w p, t s d t v e. B, I h t y b. W i t s s u y, B, H i i t d; g n f: b, H i i t s c; b i n. F a t l c o o t e, a s e u t w; s s a t c o t S o m b.
8. Matthew 24:14	And this g o t k s b p i a t w f a w u a n, a t s t e c.
9. Matthew 24:30	And then s a t s o t S o m i h: a t s a t t o t e m, a t s s t S o m c i t c o h w p a g g.

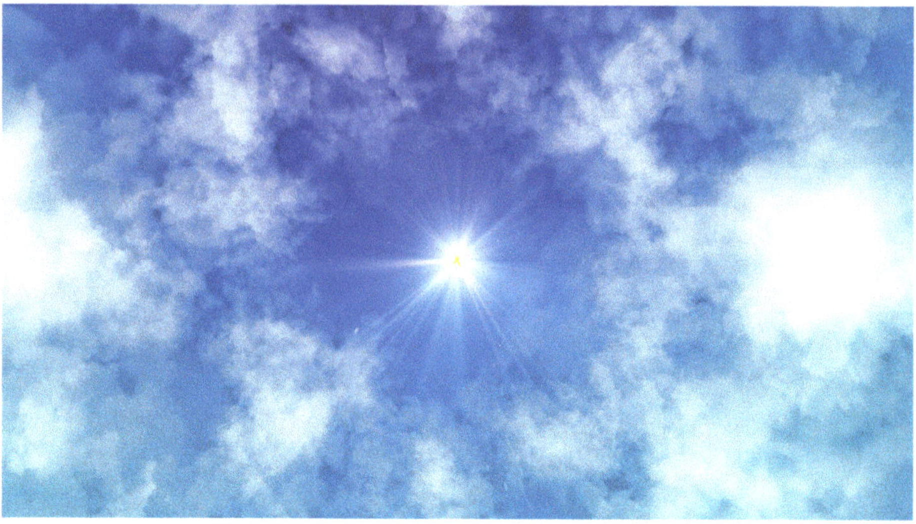

10

THE SECOND COMING—SC

1. What promise did Jesus give? John 14:1–3
2. How did Jesus go back to heaven? Acts 1:9–11
3. Who will see Jesus return? Revelation 1:7
4. Will Jesus return quietly, in secret? Matthew 24:27 (See also I Thessalonians 4:16)
5. Will our works matter to Jesus? Matthew 25:34–36, 40
6. What reward will Christ give? Revelation 22:12
7. Why will Christ come? Matthew 24:30–31
8. What happens to those who are unprepared? Revelation 6:14–17
9. When should we get ready for Jesus' return? Matthew 24:37–39, 44
10. When will He return? Matthew 24:36
11. What should we do when we see all these signs? Luke 21:25–28

10—SC

1. John 14:1–3	Let not y h b t: y b i G, b a i M. I M F h a m m: i i w n s, I w h t y. I g t p a p f y. A i I g a p a p f y, I w c a, a r y u M; t w I a, t y m b a.
2. Acts 1:9–11	And when H h s t t, w t b, H w t u; a a c r H o o t s. A w t l s t h a H w u, b, t m s b t i w a; W a s, y m o G, w s y g u i h? T s J, w i t u f y i h, s s c i l m a y h s H g i h.
3. Revelation 1:7	Behold He c w c; a e e s s H, a t a w p H: a a k o t e s w b o H. E s, A.
4. Matthew 24:27	For as t l c o o t e, a s e u t w; s s a t c o t S o m b. (see also I Thessalonians 4:16)
5. Matthew 24:34–36, 40	Then shall t K s u t o H r h, C, y b o M F, i t k p f y f t f o t w: F I w a h, a y g M m: I w t, a y g M d: I w a s, a y t M i: N, a y c M: I w s, a y v M: I w i p, a y c u M. T t K s a a s u t, V I s u y, I a y h d i u o o t l o t M b, y h d i u M.
6. Revelation 22:12	And, behold, I c q; a M r i w M, t g e m a a h w s b
7. Matthew 24:30–31	And then s a t s o t S o m i h: a t s a t t o t e m, a t s s t S o m c i t c o h w p a g g. A H s s H a w a g s o a t, a t s g t H e f t f w, f o e o h t t o.
8. Revelation 6:14–17	And the h d a a s w i i r t; a e m a i w m o o t p. A t k o t e, a t g m, a t r m, a t c c, a t m m, a e b, a e f m, h t i t d a i t r o t m; A s t t m a r, f o u, a h u f t f o H t s o t t, a f t w o t L: F t g d o H w i c; a w s b a t s?
9. Matthew 24:37–39, 44	But as t d o N w, s s a t c o t S o m b. F a i t d t w b t f t w e a d, m a g i m, u t d t N e i t a, A k n u t f c, a t t a a; s s a t c o t S o m b. T b y a r: f i s a h a y t n, t S o m c.

10—SC (*continued*)

10. Matthew 24:36	But of t d a h k n m, n, n t a o h, b m F o.
11. Luke 21:25–28	And there s b s i t s, a i t m, a i t s; a u t e d o n, w p; t s a t w r; M h f t f f, a f l a t t w a c o t e: f t p o t h s b s. A t s t s t S o m c i a c w p a g g. A w t t b t c t p, t l u, a l u y h; f y r d n.

11

BAPTISM—BP

1. Does God require baptism? Mark 16:16
2. How many kinds of baptism are there? Ephesians 4:5
3. What does baptism represent? Romans 6:3–4
4. What does it mean to be buried with Christ? Colossians 2:12
5. What does putting on Christ mean? Galatians 3:27
6. What is re-baptism? Acts 19:1–5
7. How did Philip baptize the Eunuch? Acts 8:36–39
8. What did Jesus do about baptism? Mark 1:9–11
9. Why was Jesus baptized? I Peter 2:21
10. Did Jesus and His disciples baptize? John 3:22–23,4:2
11. What great commission has the Lord given us? Matthew 28:19–20

11—BP

1. Mark 16:16	He that b a i b s b s; b h t b n s b d.
2. Ephesians 4:5	One Lord, o f, o b.
3. Romans 6:3–4	Know Ye n, t s m o u a w b i J C w b i H d? T w a b w H b b i d: t l a C w r u f t d b t g o T F, e s w a s w i n o l.
4. Colossians 2:12	Buried with H i b, w a y a r w H t t f o t o o G, w h r H f t d.
5. Galatians 3:27	For as m o y a h b b i C h p o C.
6. Acts 19:1–5	And it c t p, t, w A w a C, P h p t t u c c t E: a f c d, H s u t, H y r t H G s y b? A t s u h, w h n s m a h w t b a H G. A h s u t, U w t w y b? A t s, U J b. T s P, J v b w t b o r, s u t p, t t s b o H w s c a h, t i, o C J. W t h t, t w b i t n o t L J.
7. Acts 8:36–39	And as t w o t w, t c u a c w: a t e s, S, h I w; w d h m t b b? A P s, I t b w a t h, t m. A h a a s, I b t J C i t S o G. A h c t c t s s: a t w d b i t w, b P a t e; a h b h. A w t w c u o o t w, t S o t L c a P, t t e s h n m: a h w o h w r.
8. Mark 1:9–11	And it c t p i t d, t J c f N o G, a w b o J I J. A s c u o o t w, h s t h o, a t S l a d d u H: A t c a v f h, s, T a M b S, i w I a w p.
9. I Peter 2:21	For even h w y c: b C a s f u, l u a e, t y s f H s.
10. John 3:22–23	After these t c J a H d i t l o J; a t H t w t, a b. And John a w b i A n t S, b t w m w t: a t c, a w b.
10b. John 4:2	(Though Jesus H b n, b H d).
11. Matthew 28:19–20	Go ye t, a t a n, b t i t n o t F, a o t S, a o t H G: T t t o a t w I h c y: a, l, I a w y a, e u t e o t w. A.

12

THE SPIRIT OF PROPHESY—SP

1. What is the true church going to have? Revelation 12:17
2. What is the testimony of Jesus? Revelation 19:10
3. Whom does God use? II Peter 1:19–21
4. Through whom does God reveal things? Amos 3:7
5. Are there false prophets? Matthew 7:15; 1 John 4:1
6. Will false prophets be able to deceive us? Matthew 24:24
7. What is the test of a true prophet? Isaiah 8:20
8. How can we know a true prophet? Matthew 7:20
9. What happens when a prophet has a vision? Daniel 10:8–9, 17
10. Will prophecy always come true? Jeremiah 28:9 (see also Deuteronomy 18:22)
11. Why did God give us spiritual gifts? Ephesians 4:11–14
12. Will we have prophets in the last days? Acts 2:17 (see also Joel 2:28–29)

12—SP

1. Revelation 12:17	And the d w w w t w, a w t m w w t r o h s, w k t c o G, a h t t o J C.
2. Revelation 19:10	And I f a h f t w h. A h s u m, S t d i n: I a t f-s, a o t b t h t t o J: w G: f t t o J i t s o p.
3. II Peter 1:19–21	We have a a m s w o p; w y d w t y t h, a u a l t s i a d p, u t d d, a t d s a i y h: K t f, t n p o t S i o a p i. F t p c n i o t b t w o m: b h m o G s a t w m b t H G.
4. Amos 3:7	Surely the L G w d n, b H r H s u H s t p.
5. Matthew 7:15	Beware of f p, w c t y i s c, b i t a r w.
5b. I John 4:1	Beloved, believe n e s, b t t s w t a o G: b m f p a g o i t w.
6. Matthew 24:24	For there s a f C, a f p, a s s g s a w; i t, i i w p, t s d t v e.
7. Isaiah 8:20	To the l a t t t: i t s n a t t w, i i b t i n l I t.
8. Matthew 7:20	Wherefore by t f y s k t.
9. Daniel 10:8–9, 17	Therefore I w l a, a s t g v, a t r n s i m: f m c w t i m i c, a I r n s. Y h I t v o H w: a w I h t v o H w, t w I i a d s o m f, a m f t t g. F h c t s o t m L t w t m L? F a f m, s t r n s i m, n i t b l i m.
10. Jeremiah 28:9	The prophet w p o p, w t w o t p s c t p, t s t p b k, t t L h t s h. (see also Deuteronomy 18:22)
11. Ephesians 4:11–14	And He g s, a; a s, p; a s, e; a s, p a t; F t p o t s, f t w o t m, f t e o t b o C: T w a c i t u o t f, a o t k o t S o G, u a p m, u t m o t s o t f o C: T w h b n m c, t t a f, a c a w e w o d, b t s o m, a c c, w t l i w t d.
12. Acts 2:17	And it s c t p i t l d, s G, I w p o o m S u a f: a y s a y d s p, a y y m s s v, a y o m s d d. (see also Joel 2:28–29)

13

HEALTHFUL LIVING—HL

1. What was man's original diet? Genesis 1:29
2. When did man start eating vegetables? Genesis 3:18
3. When did man begin to eat flesh? Genesis 9:3–4
4. How many of each animal was spared in the flood? Genesis 7:2
5. Is all flesh clean? Deuteronomy 14:3, 6, 9
6. What is a good prescription for health? Proverbs 17:22
7. Does it matter what we eat and drink? I Corinthians 10:31
8. Is it important to control our appetite? Proverbs 23:2–3
9. What does God say about alcohol? Proverbs 23:31–32; Proverbs 20:1
10. What is our body and to whom does it belong? I Corinthians 3:16–17 (see also I Corinthians 6:19–20)
11. Whom will you serve? Romans 6:16
12. How should we present our bodies to God? Romans 12:1–2

13—HL

1. Genesis 1:29	And God s, B, I h g y e h b s, w i u t f o a t e, a e t, i t w i t f o a t y s; t y i s b f m.
2. Genesis 3:18	Thorns also a t s i b f t t; a t s e t h o t f.
3. Genesis 9:3–4	Every moving t t l s b m f y; e a t g h h I g y a t. B f w t l t w i t b t, s y n e.
4. Genesis 7:2	Of every c b t s t t t b s, t m a h f: a o b t a n c b t, t m a h f.
5. Deuteronomy 14:3, 6, 9	Thou shalt n e a a t. ... A e b t p t h, a c t c i t c, a c t c a t b, t y s e. ... T y s e o a t a i t w: a t h f a s s y e.
6. Proverbs 17:22	A merry h d g l a m: b a b s d t b.
7. I Corinthians 10:31	Whether therefore y e, o d, o w y d, d a t t g o G.
8. Proverbs 23:2–3	And put a k t t t, i t b a m g t a. B n d o h d: f t a d m.
9. Proverbs 23:31–32	Look not t u t w w i i r, w i g h c i t c, w i m i a. A t l i b l a s, a s l a a.
9b. Proverbs 20:1	Wine is a m, s d i r: a w i d t i n w.
10. I Corinthians 3:16–17	Know ye n t y a t t o G, a t t S o G d i y? I a m d t t o G, h s G d; f t t o G i h, w t y a. (see also I Corinthians 6:19–20)
11. Romans 6:16	Know ye n, t t w y y y s t o, h s y a t w y o; w o s u d, o o o u r?
12. Romans 12:1–2	I beseech y t, b, b t m o G, t y p y b a l s, h, a u G, w i y r s. A b n c t t w: b b y t b t r o y m, t y m p w i t g, a a, a p, w o G.

14

STEWARDSHIP—SS

1. Should we worry about food and clothing? Matthew 6:31–33
2. Who owns everything? Psalm 24:1
3. How do we get wealth? Deuteronomy 8:18
4. Where should our treasure be stored? Matthew 6:19–21
5. What is tithe? Leviticus 27:32
6. Is it possible to rob God? Malachi 3:8–11
7. Who receives the tithe? Numbers 18:21
8. What is the tithe for? I Corinthians 9:11–14
9. What else can we give besides tithe? Psalm 96:8
10. How much offerings should we give? Deuteronomy 16:17
11. What should be our attitude toward giving? II Corinthians 9:7

14—SS

1. Matthew 6:31–33	Therefore take n t, s, W s w e? o, W s w d? o,W-w s w b c? (F a a t t d t G s:) f y h F k t y h n o a t t. B s y f t k o G, a H r; a a t t s b a u y.
2. Psalm 24:1	The earth i t L, a t f t; t w, a t t d t.
3. Deuteronomy 8:18	But thou s r t L t G: f i i H t g t p t g w, t H m e H c w H s u t f, a i i t d.
4. Matthew 6:19–21	Lay not u f y t u e, w m a r d c, a w t b t a s: B l u f y t i h, w n m n r d c, a w t d n b t n s: F w y t i, t w y h b a.
5. Leviticus 27:32	And concerning t t o t h, o o t f, e o w p u t r, t t s b h u t L.
6. Malachi 3:8–11	Will a m r G? Y y h r m. B y s, W h w r t? I t a o. Y a c w a c: f y h r m, e t w n. B y a t t i t s, t t m b m i m h, a p m n h, s t L o h, i I w n o y t w o h, a p y o a b, t t s n b r e t r i. A I w r t d f y s, a h s n d t f o y g; n s y v c h f b t t i t f, s t L o h.
7. Numbers 18:21	And, behold, I h g t c o L a t t i I f a i, f t s w t s, e t s o t t o t c.
8. I Corinthians 9:11–14	If we h s u y s t, i i a g t i w s r y c t? I o b p o t p o y, a n w r? N w h n u t p; b s a t, l w s h t g o C. D y n k t t w m a h t l o t t o t t? A t w w a t a a p w t a? E s h t L o t t w p t g s l o t g.
9. Psalm 96:8	Give unto t L t g d u H n: b a o, a c i H c.
10. Deuteronomy 16:17	Every man s g a h i a, a t t b o t L t G w H h g t.
11. II Corinthians 9:7	Every man a a h p i h h, s l h g, n g, o o n: f G l a c g.

15

THE SANCTUARY—TS

1. Why did God tell Moses to build a sanctuary? Exodus 25:8
2. Describe the sanctuary. Hebrews 9:2–5
3. What law did Moses put in the ark? Deuteronomy 10:4–5
4. How were sins forgiven at that time? Leviticus 4:27–29
5. What happened on the Day of Atonement? Leviticus 16:8, 33–34
6. Who is the True Lamb? John 1:29
7. What did the OT sanctuary represent? Hebrews 9:24
8. Who is our High Priest? Hebrews 8:2; 9:11
9. How was sin removed? Hebrews 9:22–23
10. When did Jesus enter the most holy place in heaven? Daniel 8:14
11. How are sins forgiven today? Acts 4:12

15—TS

1. Exodus 25:8	And let t m m a s; t I m d a t.
2. Hebrews 9:2–5	For there w a t m; t f, w w t c, a t t, a t s; w i c t s. A a t s v, t t w i c t H o a; W h t g c, a t a o t c o r a w g, w w t g p t h m, a A r t b, a t t o t c. A o i t c o g s t m; o w w c n s p.
3. Deuteronomy 10:4–5	And He w o t t, a t t f w, t t c, w t L s u y i t m o o t m o t f i t d o t a: a t L g t u m. A I t m a c d f t m, a p t t i t a w I h m; a t t b, a t L c m.
4. Leviticus 4:27–29	And if a o o t c p s t i, w h d s a a o t c o t L c t w o n t b d, a b g; O i h s, w h h s, c t h k: t h s b h o, a k o t g, a f w b, f h s w h h s. A h s l h h u t h o t s o, a s t s o i t p o t b o.
5. Leviticus 16:8, 33–34	And Aaron s c l u t t g; o l f t L a t o l f t s....A h s m a a f t h s, a h s m a a f t t o t c, a f t a, a h s m a a f t p, a f a t p o t c. A t s b a e s u y, t m a a f t c o I f a t s o a y. A h d a t L c M.
6. John 1:29	The next d J s J c u h, a s, B t L o G, w t a t s o t w.
7. Hebrews 9:24	For Christ i n e i t h p m w h, w a t f o t t; b i h i, n t a i t p o G f u.
8. Hebrews 8:2	A minister o t s, a o t t t, w t L p, a n m.
8b. Hebrews 9:11	But Christ b c a h p o g t t c, b a g a m p t, n m w h, t i t s, n o t b.
9. Hebrews 9:22–23	And almost a t a b t l p w b; a w s o b i n r. I w t n t t p o t i t h s b p w t; b t h t t w b s t t.
10. Daniel 8:14	And He s u m, u t t a t h d; t s t s b c.
11. Acts 4:12	Neither is t s i a o: f t i n o n u h g a m, w w m b s.

16

THE JUDGMENT—JM

1. Is there a judgment? If so, by whom? Acts 17:30–31
2. Who will be judged? Ecclesiastes 3:17
3. Does God have a record of our lives? Ecclesiastes 12:14
4. What method does God use to judge? Revelation 20:12
5. Who will be in the book of life? Revelation 3:5
6. How are the sheep and goats different? Matthew 25:31–41
7. How many will be judged? II Corinthians 5:10
8. Are we held accountable for our actions? Romans 14:12
9. Who will take part in judging besides God? I Corinthians 6:2–3; (see also Daniel 7:22)
10. With whom does judgment begin? I Peter 4:17
11. How is God's reward distributed? Revelation 22:12

16—JM

1. Acts 17:30–31	And the t o t i G w a; b n c a m e t r: B H h a a d, i t w H w j t w i r b t M w H h o; w H h g a u a m, i t H h r H f t d.
2. Ecclesiastes 3:17	I said i m h, G s j t r a t w: f t i a t t f e p a f e w.
3. Ecclesiastes 12:14	For God s b e w i j, w e s t, w i b g, o w i b e.
4. Revelation 20:12	And I s t d, s a g, s b G; a t b w o: a a b w o, w i t b o l: a t d w j o o t t w w w i t b, a t t w.
5. Revelation 3:5	He that o, t s s b c i w r; a I w n b o h n o o t b o l, b I w c h n b M F, a b H a.
6. Matthew 25:31–41	When the S o m s c i H g, a a t h a w H, t s H s u t t o H g: A b H s b g a n: a H s s t o f a, a a s d h s f t g: A H s s t s o H r h, b t g o t l. T s t K s u t o H r h, C, y b o M F, i t k p f y f t f o t w: F I w a h, a y g M m: I w t, a y g M d: I w a s, a y t M i. N, a y c M: I w s, a y v M: I w i p, a y c u M. T s t r a H, s, L, w s w T a h, a f T? o t, a g T d? W s w T a s, a t T i? O n, a c T? O w s w T s, o i p, a c u T? A t K s a a s u t, V I s u y, I a y h d i u o o t l o t m b, y h d i u M. T s H s a u t o t l h, D f M, y c, i e f, p f t d a h a.
7. II Corinthians 5:10	For we m a a b t j s o C; t e o m r t t d i h b, a t t h h d, w i b g o b.
8. Romans 14:12	So then e o o u s g a o h t G.
9. I Corinthians 6:2–3	Do you n k t t s s j t w? a i t w s b j b y, a y u t j t s m? K y n t w s j a? h m m t t p t t l? (see also Daniel 7:22)
10. I Peter 4:17	For the t i c t j m b a t h o G: a i i f b a u, w s t e b o t t o n t g o G?
11. Revelation 22:12	And, behold, I c q; a m r i w M, t g e m a a h w s b.

17

CHURCH STANDARDS—CS

1. What principle should guide the Christian at all times? Philippians 4:8
2. Should God be glorified in every aspect of our lives? I Corinthians 10:31
3. What is God's advice to us? Ephesians 4:29–32
4. Is God concerned with the words we speak? Ephesians 5:3–4
5. What advice to married couples does He give? Ephesians 5:22, 25
6. What should be our attitude toward divorce? I Corinthians 7:10
7. How can a Christian avoid being worldly? Romans 12:1–2
8. What high standard should we have regarding jewelry? I Peter 3:3–4 (see also I Timothy 2:9–10)
9. How was the harlot woman arrayed? Revelation 17:4–5
10. Compare this woman to the one in Revelation 12:1.
11. What kind of people will be prepared for Jesus' coming? II Peter 3:13–14

17—CS

1. Philippians 4:8	Finally, brethren, w t a t, w t a h, w t a j, w t a p, w t a l, w t a o g r; i t b a v, a i t b a p, t o t t.
2. I Corinthians 10:31	Whether therefore y e, o d, o w y d, d a t t g o G.
3. Ephesians 4:29–32	Let no c c p o o y m, b t w i g t t u o e, t i m m g u t h. A g n t H S o G, w y a s u t d o r. L a b, a w, a a, a c, a e s, b p a f y, w a m. A b y k o t a, t, f o a, e a G f C s h f y.
4. Ephesians 5:3–4	But fornication, a a u, o c, l i n b o n a y, a b s; N f, n f t, n j, w a n c: b r g o t.
5. Ephesians 5:22, 25	Wives, submit y u y o h, a u t L. ... H, l y w, e a C a l t c, a g H f i.
6. I Corinthians 7:10	And unto t m I c, y n I, b t L, L n t w d f h h.
7. Romans 12:1–2	I beseech y t, b, b t m o G, t y p y b a l s, h, a u G, w i y r s. A b n c t t w: b b y t b t r o y m, t y m p w i t g, a a, a p, w o G.
8. I Peter 3:3–4	Whose adorning l i n b t o a o p t h, a o w o g, o o p o o a; B l i b t h m o t h i t w i n c, e t o o a m a q s, w i i t s o G o g p. (see also I Tim. 2:9–10)
9. Revelation 17:4–5	And the w w a i p a s c, a d w g a p s a p, h a g c i h h f o a a f o h f: A u h f w a n w, M, B T G, T M O H A A O T E.
10. Revelation 12:1	And there a a g w i h; a w c w t s, a t m u h f, a u h h a c o t s.
11. II Peter 3:13–14	Nevertheless we, a t H p, l f n h a a n e, w d r. W, b, s t y l f s t, b d t y m b f o H i p, w s, a b.

18

STATE OF THE DEAD—SD

1. What warning did God give Adam and Eve? Genesis 2:17
2. What lie did the serpent tell Eve? Genesis 3:1–4
3. Who only has immortality? I Timothy 6:14–16
4. Can a soul die? Ezekiel 18:4
5. What do the dead know? Ecclesiastes 9:5
6. What happens at death? Psalm 146:4
7. What did Jesus compare death to? John 11:11–14
8. What happens to our bodies at death? Ecclesiastes 12:7
9. What is man's spirit, according to the Bible? Job 27:3
10. How did God make man? Genesis 2:7
11. Is the grave permanent? John 5:28–29
12. When will the dead rise? 1 Thessalonians 4:16–17
13. When do we receive immortality? 1 Corinthians 15:51–55

18—SD

1. Genesis 2:17	But of t t o t k o g a e, t s n e o i: f i t d t t e t, t s s d.
2. Genesis 3:1–4	Now the s w m s t a b o t f w t L G h m. A h s u t w, Y, h G s, Y s n e o e t o t g? A t w s u t s, W m e o t f o t t o t g: B o t f o t t w i i t m o t g, G h s, Y s n e o i, n s y t i, l y d. A t s s u t w, y s n s d.
3. I Timothy 6:14–16	That thou k t c w s, u, u t a o o L J C: W i H t H s s, w i t b a o P, t K o k, a L o l; W o h i, d i t l w n m c a u; w n m h s, n c s: t w b h a p e. A.
4. Ezekiel 18:4	Behold, all s a m; a t s o t f, s a t s o t s i m: t s t s, i s d.
5. Ecclesiastes 9:5	For the l k t t s d: b t d k n a t, n h t a m a r; f t m o t i f.
6. Psalm 146:4	His breath g f, h r t h e; i t v d h t p.
7. John 11:11–14	These things s H: a a t H s u t, O f L s; b I g, t I m a h o o s. T s H d, L, i h s, h s d w. H J s o h d: b t t t H h s o t o r i s. T s J u t p, L i d.
8. Ecclesiastes 12:7	Then shall t d r t t e a i w: a t s s r u G w g i.
9. Job 27:3	All the w m b i i m, a t s o G i i m n.
10. Genesis 2:7	And the L G f m o t d o t g, a b i h n t b o l; a m b a l s.
11. John 5:28–29	Marvel not a t: f t h i c, i t w a t a i t g s h H v, A s c f; t t h d g, u t r o l; a t t h d e, u t r o d.
12. I Thessalonians 4:16–17	For the L H s d f h w a s, w t v o t a, a w t t o G: a t d i C s r f; T w w a a a r s b c u t w t i t c, t m t L i t a: a s s w e b w t L.

18—SD *(continued)*

13. I Corinthians 15:51–55	Behold, I s y a m; W s n a s, b w s a b c, I a m, i t t o a e, a t l t: f t t s s, a t d s b r i, a w s b c. F t c m p o i, a t m m p o i. S w t c s h p o i, a t m s h p o i, t s b b t p t s t i w, D i s u i v, O d, w i t s? O g, w i t v?

19

THE MILLENNIUM—ML

1. What will the wicked do at Christ's return? Revelation 6:14–17
2. What happens to the wicked? II Thessalonians 1:7–9
3. What happens to Satan at Christ's coming? Revelation 20:1–3
4. What happens to the righteous during the thousand years? Revelation 20:5–6
5. What is the second death? Revelation 20:14–15 (see Revelation 21:8)
6. What will the righteous do during the millennium? Revelation 20:4 (see also I Corinthians 6:2–3)
7. What is earth like during the millennium? Jeremiah 4:23–26
8. How does Jesus cleanse the earth? Revelation 20:7–10
9. What about God's children during and after the millennium? Revelation 21:3–4

19—ML

1. Revelation 6:14–17	And the h d a a s w i i r t; a e m a i w m o o t p. A t k o t e, a t g m, a t r m, a t c c, a t m m, a e b, a e f m, h t i t d a i t r o t m; A s t t m a r, F o u, a h u f t f o H t s o t t, a f t w o t L: F t g d o H w i c; a w s b a t s?
2. II Thessalonians 1:7–9	And to y w a t r w u, w t L J s b r f h w H m a, i f f t v o t t k n G, a t o n t g o o L J C: W s b p w e d f t p o t L, a f t g o H p.
3. Revelation 20:1–3	And I s a a c d f h, h t k o t b p a a g c i h h. A h l h o t d, t o s, w i t D, a S, a b h a t y, A c h i t b p, a s h u, a s a s u h, t h s d t n n m, t t t y s b f: a a t h m b l a l s.
4. Revelation 20:5–6	But the r o t d l n a u t t y w f. T i t f r. B a h i h t h p i t f r: o s t s d h n p, b t s b p o G a o C, a s r w H a t y.
5. Revelation 20:14–15	And death a h w c i t l o f. T i t s d. A w w n f w i t b o l w c i t l o f. (see also Rev. 21:8)
6. Revelation 20:4	And I s t, a t s u t, a j w g u t: a I s t s o t t w b f t w o J, a f t w o G, a w h n w t b, n h i, n h r h m u t f, o i t h; a t l a r w C a t y. (see also I Cor. 6:2–3)
7. Jeremiah 4:23–26	I beheld t e, a l, i w w f, a v; a t h, a t h n l. I b t m, a, l, t t, a a t h m l. I b, a, l, t w n m, a a t b o t h w f. I b, a, l, t f p w a w, a a t c t w b d a t p o t L, a b H f a.
8. Revelation 20:7–10	And when t t y a e, S s b l o o h p, A s g o t d t n w a i t f q o t e, G a M, t g t t t b: t n o w i a t s o t s. A t w u o t b o t e, a c t c o t s a, a t b c: a f c d f G o o h, a d t. A t d t d t w c i t l o f a b, w t b a t f p a, a s b t d a n f e a e.
9. Revelation 21:3–4	And I h a g v o o h s, B, t t o G i w m, a H w d w t, a t s b H p, a G H s b w t, a b t G. A G s w a a t f t e; a t s b n m d, n s, n c, n s t b a m p: f t f t a p a.

20

THE LITTLE HORN—LH

1. What four beasts did Daniel see? Daniel 7:4–7
2. What did they represent? Daniel 7:17
3. What was the little horn to do? Daniel 7:8
4. What is blasphemy? Mark 2:7
5. How does John describe blasphemy? John 10:33
6. What did the little horn do to God's people? Daniel 7:20–21
7. What does the little horn try to do to God's law? Daniel 7:25
8. Read Paul's description of this apostate power. Acts 20:29–30
9. Who is this power? II Thessalonians 2:3–4
10. Which kingdom will prevail? Daniel 7:27

20—LH

1. Daniel 7:4–7	*First beast*—The first w l a l, a h e w: I b t t w t w p, a i w l u f t e, a m s u t f a a m, a a m h w g t i.
	Second beast—And behold a b, a s, l t a b, a i r u i o o s, a i h t r i t m o i b t t o i: a t s t u i, A, d m f.
	Third beast—After this I b, a l a, l a l, w h u t b o i f w o a f; t b h a f h; a d w g t i.
	Fourth beast—After this I s i t n v, a b a f b, d a t, a s e; a i h g i t: i d a b i p, a s t r w t f o i: a i w d f a t b t w b i; a i h t h.
2. Daniel 7:17	These great b, w a f, a f k, w s a o o t e.
3. Daniel 7:8	I considered t h, a, b, t c u a t a l h, b w t w t o t f h p u b t r: a, b, i t h w e l t e o m a a m s g t.
4. Mark 2:7	Why doth t m t s b? w c f s b G o?
5. John 10:33	The Jews a H, s, F a g w w s t n; b f b; a b t t, b a m, m t G.
6. Daniel 7:20–21	And of t t h t w i h h, a o t o w c u, a b w t f; e o t h t h e, a a m t s v g t, w l w m s t h f. I b, a t s h m w w t s, a p a t.
7. Daniel 7:25	And he s s g w a t m H, a s w o t s o t m H, a t t c t a l: a t s b g i h h u a t a t a t d o t.
8. Acts 20:29–30	For I k t, t a m d s g w e i a y, n s t f. A o y o s s m a, s p t, t d a d a t.
9. II Thessalonians 2:3–4	Let no m d y b a m: f t d s n c, e t c a f a f, a t m o s b r, t s o p; W o a e h a a t i c G, o t i w; s t h a G s i t t o G, s h t h i G.
10. Daniel 7:27	And the k a d, a t g o t k u t w h, s b g t t p o t s o t m H, w k i a e k, a a d s s a o H.

21

MARK OF THE BEAST—MB

1. Where in the Bible is the seal of God found? Exodus 20:8–11
2. Why do we keep the Sabbath? Exodus 31:16–17
3. Who are the children of Israel? Galatians 3:26–29
4. Who will have the seal of God? Revelation 7:2–3
5. Who are the 144,000? Revelation 7:4 (see also verse 14)
6. What are the two great powers? Revelation 12:17
7. Who is the beast power? Revelation 13:1–3 (see verses 4–8)
8. Is this beast in operation today? II Thessalonians 2:3–4
9. Where is the mark of the beast found? Revelation 13:15–18
10. What is the final fate of the beast? Revelation 20:10

21—MB

1. Exodus 20:8–11	Remember the S d t k i h. S d s t l, a d a t w: B t s d i t S o t L t G: i i t s n d a w, t, n t s, n t d, t m, n t m, n t c, n t s t i w t g: F i s d t L m h a e, t s, a a t i t i, a r t s d: w t L b t S d, a h i.
2. Exodus 31:16–17	Wherefore the c o I s k t S, t o t S t t g, f a p c. I i a s b M a t c o I f e: f i s d t L m h a e, a o t s d H r, a w r.
3. Galatians 3:26–29	For ye a a t c o G b f i C J. F a m o y a h b b i C h p o C. T i n J n G, t i n b n f, t i n m n f: f y a a o i C J. A i y b C, t a y A s, a h a t t p.
4. Revelation 7:2–3	And I s a a a f t e, h t s o t l G: a h c w a l v t t f a, t w i w g t h t e a t s, S, H n t e, n t s, n t t, t w h s t s o o G i t f.
5. Revelation 7:4	And I h t n o t w w s: a t w s a h a f a f t o a t t o t c o I. (see also verse 14)
6. Revelation 12:17	And the d w w w t w, a w t m w w t r o h s, w k t c o G, a h t t o J C.
7. Revelation 13:1–3	And I s u t s o t s, a s a b r u o o t s, h s h a t h, a u h h t c, a u h h t n o b. A t b w I s w l u a l, a h f w a t f o a b, a h m a t m o a l: a t d g h h p, a h s, a g a. A I s o o h h a i w w t d; a h d w w h: a a t w w a t b. (see also verses. 4–8)
8. II Thessalonians 2:3–4	Let no m d y b a m: f t d s n c, e t c a f a f, a t m o s b r, t s o p; W o a e h a a t i c G, o t i w; s t h a G s i t t o G, s h t h i G.
9. Revelation 13:15–18	And he h p t g l u t i o t b, t t i o t b s b s, a c t a m a w n w t i o t b s b k. A h c a, b s a g, r a p, f a b, t r a m i t r h, o i t f: A t n m m b o s, s h t h t m, o t n o t b, o t n o h n. H i w. L h t h u c t n o t b: f i i t n o a m; a h n i s h t a s.
10. Revelation 20:10	And the d t d t w c i t l o f a b, w t b a t f p a, a s b t d a n f e a e.

22

THREE ANGELS' MESSAGES—TA

1. What is the first angel's message? Revelation 14:6–7
2. What does the first angel's message point to? Exodus 31:16–17
3. What is the second angel's message? Revelation 14:8
4. Who are the dragon, beast, and false prophet? Revelation 13:3–5; Revelation 16:13–14 (see also Revelation 17:8–9)
5. What is Babylon? Revelation 18:2
6. What is the third angel's message? Revelation 14:9–11
7. Who is the "image of the beast"? Revelation 13:11–12
8. What does the beast give the "image of the beast" power to do? Revelation 13:15–18
9. Who gets victory over the beast? Revelation 14:12
10. What will be the result to those who overcome? Revelation 15:2

22—TA

1. Revelation 14:6–7	And I s a a f i t m o h, h t e g t p u t t d o t e, a t e n, a k, a t, a p, S w a l v, F G, a g g t H; f t h o H j i c: a w H t m h a e, a t s, a t f o w.
2. Exodus 31: 16–17	Wherefore the c o I s k t S, t o t S t t g, f a p c. I i a s b M a t c o I f e: f i s d t L m h a e, a o t s d H r, a w r.
3. Revelation 14:8	And there f a a, s, B i f, i f, t g c, b s m a n d o t w o t w o h f.
4. Revelation 13:3–5	And I s o o h h a i w w t d; a h d w w h: a a t w w a t b. A t w t d w g p u t b: a t w t b, s, W i l u t b? w i a t m w w h? A t w g u h a m s g t a b; a p w g u h t c f a t m.
4b. Revelation 16:13–14	And I s t u s l f c o o t m o t d, a o o t m o t b, a o o t m o t f p. F t a t s o d, w m, w g f u t k o t e a o t w w, t g t t t b o t g d o G A. (see also Revelation 17:8–9)
5. Revelation 18:2	And he c m w a s v, s, B t g i f, i f, a i b t h o d, a t h o e f s, a a c o e u a h b.
6. Revelation 14:9–11	And the t a f t, s w a l v, I a m w t b a h i, a r h m i h f, o i h h, T s s d o t w o t w o G, w i p o w m i t c o h i; a h s b t w f a b i t p o t h a, a i t p o t L: A t s o t t a u f e a e: a t h n r d n n, w w t b a h i, a w r t m o h n.
7. Revelation 13:11–12	And I b a b c u o o t e; a h h t h l a l, a h s a a d. A h e a t p o t f b b h, a c t e a t w d t t w t f b, w d w w h.
8. Revelation 13:15–18	And he h p t g l u t i o t b, t t i o t b s b s, a c t a m a w n w t i o t b s b k. A h c a, b s a g, r a p, f a b, t r a m i t r h, o i t f: A t n m m b o s, s h t h t m, o t n o t b, o t n o h n. H i w. L h t h u c t n o t b: f i i t n o a m; a h n i S h t a s.
9. Revelation 14:12	Here is t p o t s: h a t t k t c o G, a t f o J.
10. Revelation 15:2	And I s a i w a s o g m w f: a t t h g t v o t b, a o h i, a o h m, a o t n o h n, s o t s o g, h t h o G.

23

SEVEN LAST PLAGUES—LP

1. What is the first plague at the end time? Revelation 16:1–2
2. What is the second plague? Revelation 16:3
3. What is the third plague? Revelation 16:4
4. Why does God send plagues of blood? Revelation 16:5–6
5. What is the fourth plague? Revelation 16:8
6. What is the fifth plague? Revelation 16:10
7. Describe the sixth plague. Revelation 16:12
8. What events take place during the seventh plague? Revelation 16:17–21
9. Who receives these plagues? Revelation 17:1, 3–6 (see also Revelation 18:2, 8)
10. Will the plagues fall on God's people? Revelation 18:4

23—LP

1. Revelation 16:1–2 — And I h a g v o o t t s t t s a, G y w, a p o t v o t w o G u t e. A t f w, a p o h v u t e; a t f a n a g s u t m w h t m o t b, a u t w w h i.

2. Revelation 16:3 — And the s a p o h v u t s; a i b a t b o a d m: a e l s d i t s.

3. Revelation 16:4 — And the t a p o h v u t r a f o w; a t b b.

4. Revelation 16:5–6 — And I h t a o t w s, T a r O L, w a, a w, a s b, b T h j t. F t h s t b o s a p, a T h g t b t d; f t a w.

5. Revelation 16:8 — And the f a p o h v u t s; a p w g u h t s m w f.

6. Revelation 16:10 — And the f a p o h v u t s o t b; a h k w f o d; a t g t t f p.

7. Revelation 16:12 — And the s a p o h v u t g r E; a t w t w d u, t t w o t k o t e m b p.

8. Revelation 16:17–21 — And the s a p o h v i t a; a t c a g v o o t t o h, f t t, s, I i d. A t w v, a t, a l; a t w a g e, s a w n s m w u t e, s m a e, a s g. A t g c w d i t p, a t c o t n f: a g B c i r b G, t g u h t c o t w o t f o H w. A e i f a, a t m w n f. A t f u m a g h o o h, e s a t w o a t: a m b G b o t p o t h; f t p t w e g.

9. Revelation 17:1, 3–6 — And there c o o t s a w h t s v, a t w m, s u m, C h; I w s u t t j o t g w t s u m w…S h c m a i t s i t w: a I s a w s u a s c b, f o n o b, h s h a t h. A t w w a i p a s c, a d w g a p s a p, h a g c i h h f o a a f o h f: A u h f w a n w, M, B T G, T M O H A A O T E. A I s t w d w t b o t s, a w t b o t m o J: a w I s h, I w w g a. (See also Rev. 18:2, 8)

10. Revelation 18:4 — And I h a v f h, s, “C o o h, m p, t y b n p o h s, a t y r n o h p.”

24

TRUST and OBEY—TO

1. What should be our daily prayer? Psalm 139:23–24
2. How well does the Lord know us? Luke 12:7
3. Why does God want us to study His Word? II Timothy 2:15 (See also Ephesians 6:11)
4. What should we seek first? Matthew 6:33
5. What happens when we seek God? Matthew 7:7–8
6. What promise does Jesus give if we obey? John 14:14, 23
7. How do we know we love God? I John 5:1–4
8. Can we ignore what is good? James 4:17
9. Can we obey God through our own strength? Philippians 4:13
10. What can we do to overcome Satan? James 4:7
11. What is the result of obedience to God's commandments? Revelation 22:14

24—TO

1. Psalm 139:23–24	Search me, O G, a k m h: t m, a k m t: A s i t b a w w i m, a l m i t w e.
2. Luke 12:7	But even t v h o y h a a n. F n t: y a o m v t m s.
3. II Timothy 2:15	Study to s t a u G, a w t n n t b a, r d t w o t. (see also Ephesians 6:11)
4. Matthew 6:33	But seek y f t k o G, a h r; a a t t s b a u y.
5. Matthew 7:7–8	Ask, and i s b g y; s, a y s f; k, a i s b o u y: F e o t a r; a h t s f; a t h t k i s b o.
6. John 14:14, 23	If ye s a a t i M n, I w d i....J a a s u h, I a m l M, h w k M w: a M F w l h, a W w c u h, a m O a w h.
7. I John 5:1–4	Whosoever believeth t J i t C i b o G: a e o t l h t b l h a t i b o h. B t w k t w l t c o G, w w l G, a k H c. F t i t l o G, t w k H c: a H c a n g. F w i b o G o t w: a t i t v t o t w, e o f.
8. James 4:17	Therefore to h t k t d g, a d i n, t h i i s.
9. Philippians 4:13	I can d a t t C w s m.
10. James 4:7	Submit yourselves t t G. R t d, a h w f f y.
11. Revelation 22:14	Blessed are t t d H c, t t m h r t t t o l, a m e i t t g i t c.

25

THE TRUE CHURCH—TC

1. What is the church likened to? Jeremiah 6:2
2. How is the pure woman (or church) described? Revelation 12:1–2
3. What kind of woman is described in Revelation 17:3–6?
4. What happened to the pure woman? Revelation 12:6, 14
5. Who is the man child? Revelation 12:5 (see also Acts 1:9–11)
6. Name the two identifying marks of the true church? Revelation 14:12
7. How does Revelation 14:12 compare to Revelation 12:17?
8. What is the testimony of Jesus? Revelation 19:10
9. What does God say to our leaders? Jeremiah 23:1–4
10. What is God saying to you and me today? Revelation 18:4

25—TC

1. Jeremiah 6:2	I have l t d o Z t a c a d w.
2. Revelation 12:1–2	And there a a g w i h; a w c w t s, a t m u h f, a u h h a c o t s: A s b w c c, t i b, a p t b d.
3. Revelation 17:3–6	So he c m a i t s i t w: a I s a w s u a s c b, f o n o b, h s h a t h. A t w w a i p a s c, a d w g a p s a p, h a g c i h h f o a a f o h f: A u h f w a n w, M, B T G, T M O H A A O T E. A I s t w d w t b o t s, a w t b o t m o J: a w I s h, I w w g a.
4. Revelation 12:6, 14	And the w f i t w, w s h a p p o G, t t s f h t a t t h a t d...A t t w w g t w o a g e t s m f i t w, i h p, w s i n f a t, a t, a h a t, f t f o t s.
5. Revelation 12:5	And she b f a m c, w w t r a n w a r o i: a h c w c u u G, a t H t. (see also Acts 1:9–11)
6. Revelation 14:12	Here is t p o t s: h a t t k t c o G, a t f o J.
7. Revelation 12:17	And the d w w w t w, a w t m w w t r o h s, w k t c o G, a h t t o J C.
8. Revelation 19:10	And I f a h f t w h. A h s u m, S t d i n: I a t f-s, a o t b t h t t o J: w G: f t t o J i t s o p.
9. Jeremiah 23:1–4	Woe be u t p t d a s t s o m p! s t L. T t s t L G o I a t p t f m p; Y h s m f, a d t a, a h n v t: b, I w v u y t e o y d, s t L. A I w g t r o m f o o a c w I h d t, a w b t a t t f; a t s b f a i. A I w s u s o t w s f t: a t s f n m, n b d, n s t b l, s t L.
10. Revelation 18:4	And I h a v f h, s, C o o h, m p, t y b n p o h s, a t y r n o h p.

BIBLE STUDY ANSWERS

Using the King James Version

1—Inspiration of the Bible

1. **John 14:6**: Jesus saith unto him, I am the way, the truth, and the life; no man cometh unto the Father, but by me.
2. **John 17:17**: Sanctify them through Thy truth, Thy word is truth.
3. **II Timothy 3:15–17**: And that from a child thou hast known the holy scriptures, which are able to make thee wise unto salvation through faith which is in Christ Jesus. *16* All scripture is given by inspiration of God, and is profitable for doctrine, for reproof, for correction, for instruction in righteousness: *17* That the man of God may be perfect, thoroughly furnished unto all good works.
4. **II Peter 1:21**: For the prophecy came not in old times by the will of man, but holy men of God spake as they were moved by the Holy Ghost.
5. **Romans 15:4**: For whatsoever things were written aforetime were written for our learning, that we through patience and comfort of the scriptures might have hope.
6. **Luke 24:27**: And beginning at Moses and all the prophets, He expounded unto them in all the scriptures the things concerning Himself.
7. **Matthew 4:4**: But He answered and said, It is written, man shall not live by bread alone, but by every word that proceedeth out of the mouth of God.
8. **John 6:63**: It is the Spirit that quickeneth; the flesh profiteth nothing; the words that I speak unto you, they are spirit, and they are life.
9. **Psalm 119:11**: Thy word have I hid in mine heart that I might not sin against Thee.
10. **Psalm 119:105**: Thy word is a lamp unto my feet and a light unto my path.

2—Origin of Sin

1. **I John 3:8**: He that committeth sin is of the devil; for the devil sinneth from the beginning...
2. **Ezekiel 28:14–15**: Thou art the anointed cherub that covereth; and I have set thee so: thou wast upon the holy mountain of God... *15* Thou wast perfect in thy ways from the day that thou wast created, till iniquity was found in thee.
3. **Isaiah 14:12–14**: How art thou fallen from heaven, O Lucifer, son of the morning! how art thou cut down to the ground, which didst weaken the nations! *13* For thou hast said in thine heart, I will ascend into heaven, I will exalt my throne above the stars of God...*14* I will be like the most High.
4. **Revelation 12:7–9**: And there was war in heaven: Michael and His angels fought against the dragon; and the dragon fought and his angels, *8* And prevailed not; neither was their place found any more in heaven. *9* And the great dragon was cast out, that old serpent, called the Devil, and Satan, which deceiveth the whole world; he was cast out into the earth, and his angels were cast out with him.
5. **Revelation 12:12**: Woe to the inhabiters of the earth and of the sea! for the devil is come down unto you, having great wrath, because he knoweth that he hath but a short time.
6. **I Peter 5:8**: Be sober, be vigilant; because your adversary the devil, as a roaring lion, walketh about, seeking whom he may devour.
7. **Genesis 2:17**: But of the tree of the knowledge of good and evil, thou shalt not eat of it: for in the day that thou eatest thereof thou shalt surely die.
8. **Genesis 3:1–4**: Now the serpent was more subtle than any beast of the field which the Lord God had made. And he said unto the woman, Yea, hath God said, Ye shall not eat of every tree of the garden? *2* And the woman said unto the serpent, We may eat of the fruit of the trees of the garden: *3* But of the fruit of the tree which is in the midst of the garden, God hath said, Ye shall not eat of it, neither shall ye touch it, lest ye die. *4* And the serpent said unto the woman, Ye shall not surely die.
9. **I John 3:4**: Whosoever committeth sin transgresseth also the law: for sin is the transgression of the law.
10. **Romans 3:23**: For all have sinned, and come short of the glory of God.

11. **Romans 3:24**: Being justified freely by His grace through the redemption that is in Christ Jesus. **John 3:16**: For God so loved the world, that He gave His only begotten Son, that whosoever believeth in Him should not perish, but have everlasting life.
12. **Nahum 1:9**: What do ye imagine against the Lord? He will make an utter end: affliction shall not rise up the second time.

3—Salvation

1. **Acts 16:30**: And brought them out, and said, Sirs, what must I do to be saved?
2. **Acts 16:31:** And they said, Believe on the Lord Jesus Christ, and thou shalt be saved, and thy house. **Mark 16:16**: He that believeth and is baptized shall be saved; but he that believeth not shall be damned.
3. **Romans 6:23**: For the wages of sin is death but the gift of God is eternal life through Jesus Christ our Lord.
4. **Romans 5:8**: But God commendeth His love toward us, in that, while we were yet sinners, Christ died for us.
5. **Romans 3:23–24**: For all have sinned and come short of the glory of God; *24* Being justified freely by His grace through the redemption that is in Christ Jesus.
6. **I John 4:9–11**: In this was manifested the love of God toward us, because that God sent His only begotten Son into the world, that we might live through Him. *10* Herein is love, not that we loved God, but that He loved us, and sent His Son to be the propitiation for our sins. *11* Beloved, if God so loved us, we ought also to love one another.
7. **John 3:16:** For God so loved the world, that He gave His only begotten Son, that whosoever believeth in Him should not perish, but have everlasting life.
8. **John 3:3–5**: Jesus answered and said unto him, Verily, verily, I say unto thee, Except a man be born again, he cannot see the kingdom of God. *4* Nicodemus saith unto Him, How can a man be born when he is old? Can he enter the second time into his mother's womb, and be born? *5* Jesus answered, Verily, verily, I say unto thee, Except a man be born of water and of the Spirit, he cannot enter into the kingdom of God.
9. **I John 1:9**: If we confess our sins, He is faithful and just to forgive us our sins, and to cleanse us from all unrighteousness.
10. **II Corinthians 5:17**: Therefore if any man be in Christ, he is a new creature: old things are passed away; behold, all things are become new. *(see also Romans 6:6)*

11. **John 1:12**: But as many as received Him, to them gave He power to become the sons of God, even to them that believe on His name.
12. **Revelation 3:20**: Behold, I stand at the door, and knock: if any man hear my voice, and open the door, I will come in to him, and will sup with him, and he with Me.

4—Heaven and New Earth

1. **John 14:1–3**: Let not your heart be troubled: ye believe in God, believe also in me. *2* In my Father's house are many mansions: if it were not so, I would have told you. I go to prepare a place for you. *3* And if I go and prepare a place for you, I will come again, and receive you unto myself; that where I am, there ye may be also.
2. **Hebrews 11:10**: For he looked for a city which hath foundations, whose builder and maker is God.
3. **I Corinthians 2:9**: But as it is written, Eye hath not seen, nor ear heard, neither have entered into the heart of man, the things which God hath prepared for them that love Him.
4. **Revelation 21:1–4:** And I saw a new heaven and a new earth: for the first heaven and the first earth were passed away; and there was no more sea. *2* And I John saw the holy city, new Jerusalem, coming down from God out of heaven, prepared as a bride adorned for her husband. *3* And I heard a great voice out of heaven saying, Behold, the tabernacle of God is with men, and He will dwell with them, and they shall be His people, and God Himself shall be with them, and be their God. *4* And God shall wipe away all tears from their eyes; and there shall be no more death, neither sorrow, nor crying, neither shall there be any more pain: for the former things are passed away.
5. **Revelation 21:10–11, 21:** And he carried me away in the spirit to a great and high mountain, and shewed me the great city, the holy Jerusalem, descending out of heaven from God, *11* Having the glory of God: and her light was like unto a stone most precious, even like a jasper stone, clear as crystal; …*21* And the twelve gates were twelve pearls: every several gate was of one pearl: and the street of the city was pure gold, as it were transparent glass.
6. **Revelation 22:1–2:** And he showed me a pure river of water of life, clear as crystal, proceeding out of the throne of God and of the Lamb. *2* In the midst of the street of it, and on either side of the river, was there the tree of life, which bare twelve manner of fruits, and yielded her fruit every month: and the leaves of the tree were for the healing of the nations.
7. **Isaiah 11:6–9**: The wolf also shall dwell with the lamb, and the leopard shall lie down with the kid; and the calf and the young lion and the fatling together; and a little child shall lead them. *7* And the cow and the

bear shall feed; their young ones shall lie down together: and the lion shall eat straw like the ox. *8* And the suckling child shall play on the hole of the asp, and the weaned child shall put his hand on the cockatrice den. *9* They shall not hurt nor destroy in all my holy mountain: for the earth shall be full of the knowledge of the Lord, as the waters cover the sea.

8. **Isaiah 65:21–22**: And they shall build houses, and inhabit them; and they shall plant vineyards, and eat the fruit of them. *22* They shall not build, and another inhabit; they shall not plant, and another eat: for as the days of a tree are the days of my people, and mine elect shall long enjoy the work of their hands.
9. **Isaiah 33:24**: And the inhabitant shall not say, I am sick: the people that dwell therein shall be forgiven their iniquity.
10. **I Corinthians 13:12**: For now we see through a glass, darkly; but then face to face: now I know in part; but then shall I know even as also I am known.
11. **Revelation 22:14**: Blessed are they that do His commandments, that they may have right to the tree of life, and may enter in through the gates into the city.

5—God's Law

1. **Exodus 31:18**: And He (God) gave unto Moses, when He had made an end of communing with him upon Mount Sinai, two tables of testimony, tables of stone, written with the finger of God.
2. **Romans 3:20**: Therefore by the deeds of the law there shall no flesh be justified in His sight: for by the law is the knowledge of sin.
3. **Romans 4:15**: Because the law worketh wrath: for where no law is, there is no transgression.
4. **I John 3:4**: Whosoever committeth sin transgresseth also the law: for sin is the transgression of the law.
5. **Ecclesiastes 12:13**: Let us hear the conclusion of the whole matter: Fear God, and keep His commandments: for this is the whole duty of man.
6. **Psalm 111:7–8**: The works of His hands are verity and judgment; all His commandments are sure. *8* They stand fast forever and ever, and are done in truth and uprightness.
7. **Romans 7:12**: Wherefore the law is holy, and the commandment holy, and just, and good.
8. **Matthew 5:17–19**: Think not that I am come to destroy the law, or the prophets: I am not come to destroy, but to fulfill. *18* For verily I say unto you, Till heaven and earth pass, one jot or one tittle shall in no wise pass from the law, till all be fulfilled. *19* Whosoever therefore shall break one of these least commandments, and shall teach men so, he shall be called the least in the kingdom of heaven: but whosoever shall do and teach them, the same shall be called great in the kingdom of heaven.
9. **Matthew 22:36–40**: Master, which is the great commandment in the law? *37* Jesus said unto him, Thou shalt love the Lord thy God with all thy heart, and with all thy soul, and with all thy mind. *38* This is the first and great commandment. *39* And the second is like unto it. Thou shalt love thy neighbor as thyself. *40* On these two commandments hang all the law and the prophets. {*The first four commandments show our love for God; the last six show our love for mankind.*}
10. **James 2:10**: For whosoever shall keep the whole law, and yet offend in one point, he is guilty of all.
11. **I John 5:1–3**: Whosoever believeth that Jesus is the Christ is born of God: and every one that loveth him that begat loveth him also that is

begotten of Him. *2* By this we know that we love the children of God, when we love God, and keep His commandments. *3* For this is the love of God, that we keep His commandments: and His commandments are not grievous.

12. **I John 2:3–6**: And hereby we do know that we know Him, if we keep His commandments. *4* He that saith, I know Him, and keepeth not His commandments, is a liar, and the truth is not in him. *5* But whoso keepeth His word, in him verily is the love of God perfected: hereby know we that we are in Him. *6* He that saith he abideth in Him ought himself also so to walk, even as He walked. **John 14:15:** If ye love me, keep my commandments.
13. **Luke 16:17**: And it is easier for heaven and earth to pass, than one tittle of the law to fail.

6—God's Sabbath

1. **Genesis 2:1–3**: Thus the heavens and the earth were finished, and all the host of them. *2* And on the seventh day God ended His work which He had made; and He rested on the seventh day from all His work which He had made. *3* And God blessed the seventh day, and sanctified it: because that in it He had rested from all His work which God created and made.
2. **Exodus 20:8–11**: Remember the Sabbath day, to keep it holy. *9* Six days shalt thou labour, and do all thy work: *10* But the seventh day is the Sabbath of the Lord thy God: in it thou shalt not do any work, thou, nor thy son, nor thy daughter, thy manservant, nor thy maidservant, nor thy cattle, nor thy stranger that is within thy gates: *11* For in six days the Lord made heaven and earth, the sea , and all that in them is, and rested the seventh day: wherefore the Lord blessed the Sabbath day, and hallowed it.
3. **Ezekiel 20:12, 20**: Moreover also I gave them My Sabbaths, to be a sign between Me and them, that they might know that I am the Lord that sanctify them. … *20* And hallow My Sabbaths; and they shall be a sign between Me and you, that ye may know that I am the Lord your God.
4. **Luke 4:16**: And He came to Nazareth, where He had been brought up: and, as His custom was, He went into the synagogue on the Sabbath day, and stood up for to read.
5. **Acts 17:2**: And Paul, as his manner was, went in unto them, and three Sabbath days reasoned with them out of the Scriptures.
6. **Luke 23:56**: And they returned, and prepared spices and ointments; and rested the Sabbath day according to the commandment.
7. **Isaiah 66:22–23**: For as the new heavens and the new earth, which I will make, shall remain before Me, saith the Lord, so shall your seed and your name remain. *23* And it shall come to pass, that from one new moon to another, and from one Sabbath to another, shall all flesh come to worship before Me, saith the Lord.
8. **Mark 2:27–28:** And He said unto them, The Sabbath was made for man, and not man for the Sabbath: *28* Therefore the Son of man is Lord also of the Sabbath.
9. **Isaiah 58:13–14**: If thou turn away thy foot from the Sabbath, from doing thy pleasure on My holy day; and call the Sabbath a delight,

the holy of the Lord, honourable; and shalt honour Him, not doing thy own ways, nor finding thine own pleasure, nor speaking thine own words: *14* Then shalt thou delight thyself in the Lord; and I will cause thee to ride upon the high places of the earth, and feed thee with the heritage of Jacob thy father: for the mouth of the Lord hath spoken it.

10. **James 2:10**: For whosoever shall keep the whole law, and yet offend in one point, he is guilty of all.

7—How to Keep the Sabbath

1. **Exodus 20:8**: Remember the Sabbath day, to keep it holy.
2. **Genesis 1:5, 13, 31**: And the evening and the morning were the first day. … *13* And the evening and the morning were the third day. … *31* And the evening and the morning were the sixth day.
3. **Leviticus 23:32**: It shall be unto you a Sabbath of rest, and ye shall afflict your souls: in the ninth day of the month at even, from even unto even, shall ye celebrate your Sabbath.
4. **Mark 15:42**: And now when the even was come, because it was the preparation, that is, the day before the Sabbath.
5. **Exodus 16:29–30**: See, for the Lord hath given you the Sabbath, therefore He giveth you on the sixth day the bread of two days; abide ye every man in his place, let no man go out of his place on the seventh day. *30* So the people rested on the seventh day.
6. **Nehemiah 13:16–18**: There dwelt men of Tyre also therein, which brought fish, and all manner of ware, and sold on the Sabbath unto the children of Judah, and in Jerusalem. *17* Then I contended with the nobles of Judah, and said unto them, What evil thing is this that ye do, and profane the Sabbath day? *18* Did not your fathers thus, and did not our God bring all this evil upon us, and upon this city? yet ye bring more wrath upon Israel by profaning the Sabbath.
7. **Isaiah 58:12–14**: And they that shall be of thee shall build the old waste places: thou shalt raise up the foundations of many generations; and thou shalt be called, The repairer of the breach, The restorer of paths to dwell in. *13* If thou turn away thy foot from the Sabbath, from doing thy pleasure on My holy day; and call the Sabbath a delight, the holy of the Lord, honourable; and shalt honour Him, not doing thy own ways, nor finding thine own pleasures, nor speaking thine own words: *14* Then shalt thou delight thyself in the Lord; and I will cause thee to ride upon the high places of the earth, and feed thee with the heritage of Jacob thy father: for the mouth of the Lord hath spoken it.
8. **Matthew 12:10–13**: And, behold, there was a man which had his hand withered, And they asked him, saying, is it lawful to heal on the Sabbath days? that they might accuse him. *11* And He said unto them, What man shall there be among you, that shall have one sheep, and if it fall into a pit on the Sabbath day, will he not lay hold on it, and lift it out? *12* How much then is a man better than a sheep? Wherefore it

is lawful to do well on the Sabbath days. *13* Then saith he to the man, Stretch forth thine hand. And he stretched it forth; and it was restored whole, like as the other.

9. **Ezekiel 20:12, 20**: Moreover also I gave them My Sabbaths, to be a sign between Me and them, that they might know that I am the Lord that sanctify them. … *20* And hallow My Sabbaths; and they shall be a sign between Me and you, that ye may know that I am the Lord your God.

8—The First Day

1. **Matthew 28:1**: In the end of the Sabbath, as it began to dawn toward the first day of the week, came Mary Magdalene and the other Mary to see the sepulchre.
2. **Mark 16:2, 9**: And very early in the morning the first day of the week, they came unto the sepulchre at the rising of the sun. … *9* Now when Jesus was risen early the first day of the week, He appeared first to Mary Magdalene, out of whom He had cast seven devils.
3. **Luke 24:1:** Now upon the first day of the week, very early in the morning, they came unto the sepulchre, bringing the spices which they had prepared, and certain others with them.
4. **John 20:1**: The first day of the week cometh Mary Magdalene early, when it was yet dark, unto the sepulchre, and seeth the stone taken away from the sepulchre.
5. **Genesis 1:3–5**: And God said, Let there be light: and there was light. *4* And God saw the light, that it was good: and God divided the light from the darkness. *5* And God called the light Day, and the darkness He called Night. And the evening and the morning were the first day.
6. **John 20:19**: Then the same day at evening, being the first day of the week, when the doors were shut where the disciples were assembled for fear of the Jews, came Jesus and stood in the midst, and saith unto them, Peace be unto you.
7. **I Corinthians 16:2**: Upon the first day of the week let every one of you lay by him in store, as God hath prospered him, that there be no gatherings when I come. {*Paul asked the believers to prepare their offerings on the first day of the week so that when he came the money would be ready for him to collect.*}
8. **Acts 20:7**: And upon the first day of the week, when the disciples came together to break bread, Paul preached unto them, ready to depart on the morrow; and continued his speech until midnight. {*See #9 for explanation of the term, "breaking bread"*}
9. **Acts 2:46**: And they, continuing daily with one accord in the temple, and breaking bread from house to house, did eat their meat with gladness and singleness of heart. {*Breaking bread = eating food*}
10. **Matthew 15:9**: But in vain they do worship Me, teaching for doctrines the commandments of men.

11. **Revelation 1:10**: I was in the Spirit on the Lord's day, and heard behind me a great voice, as of a trumpet.
12. **Mark 2:27–28**: And He said unto them, The Sabbath was made for man, and not man for the Sabbath: *28* Therefore <u>the Son of man is Lord also of the Sabbath</u>. *(see also Matthew 12:8)*

9—Signs of His Coming

1. **Matthew 24:3–8**: And as He sat upon the Mount of Olives, the disciples came unto Him privately, saying, Tell us, when shall these things be? and what shall be the sign of Thy coming, and of the end of the world? *4* And Jesus answered and said unto them, Take heed that no man deceive you. *5* For many shall come in My name, saying, I am Christ; and shall deceive many. *6* And ye shall hear of wars and rumours of wars: see that ye be not troubled: for all these things must come to pass, but the end is not yet. *7* For nation shall rise against nation, and kingdom against kingdom: and there shall be famines, and pestilences, and earthquakes in divers places. *8* All these are the beginning of sorrows.
2. **Daniel 12:1, 4**: And at that time shall Michael stand up, the great prince which standeth for the children of thy people: and there shall be a time of trouble, such as never was since there was a nation even to that same time: and at that time thy people shall be delivered, everyone that shall be found written in the book. … *4* But thou, O Daniel, shut up the words, and seal the book, even to the time of the end: many shall run to and fro, and knowledge shall be increased.
3. **II Peter 3:3–5, 8–9:** Knowing this first, that there shall come in the last days scoffers, walking after their own lusts, *4* And saying, Where is the promise of His coming? for since the fathers fell asleep, all things continue as they were from the beginning of the creation. *5* For this they willingly are ignorant of, that by the word of God the heavens were of old, and the earth standing out of the water and in the water:… *8* But beloved, be not ignorant of this one thing, that one day is with the Lord as a thousand years, and a thousand years as one day. *9* The Lord is not slack concerning His promise, as some men count slackness; but is longsuffering to us-ward, not willing that any should perish, but that all should come to repentance.
4. **II Timothy 3:1–5**: This know also, that in the last days perilous times shall come. *2* For men shall be lovers of their own selves, covetous, boasters, proud, blasphemers, disobedient to parents, unthankful, unholy, *3* Without natural affection, trucebreakers, false accusers, incontinent, fierce, despisers of those that are good, *4* Traitors, heady, highminded, lovers of pleasures more than lovers of God; *5* Having

a form of godliness, but denying the power thereof: from such turn away.

5. **I Timothy 4:1–2**: Now the Spirit speaketh expressly, that in the latter times some shall depart from the faith, giving heed to seducing spirits, and doctrines of devils. *2* Speaking lies in hypocrisy; having their conscience seared with a hot iron.
6. **Matthew 24:29**: Immediately after the tribulation of those days shall the sun be darkened (5-19-1780), and the moon shall not give her light, and the stars shall fall from heaven (11-13-1833), and the powers of the heavens shall be shaken (11-1-1755, the Lisbon earthquake).
7. **Matthew 24:19–27**: And woe unto them that are with child and to them that give suck in those days! *20* But pray ye that your flight be not in the winter, neither on the Sabbath day: *21* For then shall be great tribulation, such as was not since the beginning of the world to this time, no, nor ever shall be. *22* And except those days should be shortened, there should no flesh be saved: but for the elect's sake those days shall be shortened. *23* Then if any man shall say unto you, Lo, here is Christ, or there; believe it not. *24* For there shall arise false Christs, and false prophets, and shall shew great signs and wonders; insomuch that, if it were possible, they shall deceive the very elect. *25* Behold, I have told you before. *26* Wherefore if they shall say unto you, Behold, He is in the desert; go not forth: behold, He is in the secret chambers; believe it not. *27* For as the lightning cometh out of the east, and shineth even unto the west; so shall also the coming of the Son of man be.
8. **Matthew 24:14**: And this gospel of the kingdom shall be preached in all the world for a witness unto all nations; and then shall the end come.
9. **Matthew 24:30:** And then shall appear the sign of the Son of man in heaven: and then shall all the tribes of the earth mourn, and they shall see the Son of man coming in the clouds of heaven with power and great glory.

10—The Second Coming

1. **John 14:1–3**: Let not your heart be troubled: ye believe in God, believe also in me. *2* In My Father's house are many mansions: If it were not so, I would have told you. I go to prepare a place for you. *3* And if I go and prepare a place for you, I will come again, and receive you unto Myself; that where I am, there ye may be also.
2. **Acts 1:9–11:** And when He had spoken these things, while they beheld, He was taken up; and a cloud received Him out of their sight. *10* And while they looked steadfastly toward heaven as He went up, behold, two men stood by them in white apparel; *11* Which also said, Ye men of Galilee, why stand ye gazing up into heaven: this same Jesus, which was taken up from you into heaven, shall so come in like manner as ye have seen Him go into heaven.
3. **Revelation 1:7**: Behold, He cometh with clouds; and every eye shall see Him, and they also which pierced Him: And all kindreds of the earth shall wail because of Him. Even so, Amen.
4. **Matthew 24:27**: For as the lightning cometh out of the east, and shinneth even unto the west; so shall also the coming of the Son of man be. *(see also I Thessalonians 4:16)*
5. **Matthew 25:34–36, 40:** Then shall the King say unto themon His right hand, Come, ye blessed of my Father, inherit the kingdom prepared for you from the foundation of the world: *35* For I was an hungered, and ye gave me meat: I was thirsty, and ye gave me drink: I was a stranger, and ye took me in: *36* Naked, and ye clothed me: I was sick, and ye visited me: I was in prison, and ye came unto me. … *40* Then the King shall answer and say unto them, Verily I say unto you, Inasmuch as ye have done it unto one of the least of these my brethren, ye have done it unto me.
6. **Revelation 22:12**: And, behold, I come quickly; and My reward is with Me, to give every man according as his work shall be.
7. **Matthew 24:30–31**: And then shall appear the sign of the Son of Man in heaven: and then shall all the tribes of the earth mourn, and they shall see the Son of man comig in the clouds of heaven with power and great glory. *31* And He shall send His angels with a great sound of a trumpet, and they shall gather together His elect from the four winds, from one end of heaven to the other.

8. **Revelation 6:14–17**: And the heaven departed as a scroll when it is rolled together; and every mountain and island were moved out of their places. *15* And the kings of the earth, and the great men, and the rich men, and the chief captains, and the mighty men, and every bondman, and every free man, hid themselves in the dens and in the rocks of the mountains; *16* And said to the mountains and rocks, Fall on us, and hide us from the face of Him that sitteth on the throne, and from the wrath of the Lamb: *17* For the great day of His wrath is come; and who shall be able to stand?
9. **Matthew 24:37–39, 44**: But as the days of Noe were, so shall also the coming of the Son of man be. *38* For as in the days that were before the flood they were eating and drinking, marrying and giving in marriage, until the day that Noe entered into the ark, *39* And knew not until the flood came, and took them all away; so shall also the coming of the Son of man be. …*44* Therefore be ye also ready: for in such an hour as ye think not the Son of man cometh.
10. **Matthew 24:36**: But of that day and hour knoweth no man, no, not the angels of heaven, but My Father only.
11. **Luke 21:25–28**: And there shall be signs in the sun, and in the moon, and in the stars; and upon the earth distress of nations, with perplexity; the sea and the waves roaring; *26* Men's hearts failing them for fear, and for looking after those things which are coming on the earth: for the powers of the heaven shall be shaken. *27* And then shall they see the Son of man coming in a cloud with power and great glory. *28* And when these things begin to come to pass, then look up, and lift up your heads; for your redemption draweth nigh. {*Note: Lift up your heads means to be joyful.*}

11—Baptism

1. **Mark 16:16**: He that believeth and is baptized shall be saved; but he that believeth not shall be damned.
2. **Ephesians 4:5**: One Lord, one faith, one baptism.
3. **Romans 6:3–4**: Know Ye not, that so many of us as were baptized into Jesus Christ were baptized into His death? *4* Therefore we are buried with Him by baptism into death: that like as Christ was raised up from the dead by the glory of the Father, even so we also should walk in newness of life.
4. **Colossians 2:12**: Buried with Him in baptism, wherein also ye are risen with Him through the faith of the operation of God, who hath raised Him from the dead.
5. **Galatians 3:27**: For as many of you as have been baptized into Christ have put on Christ.
6. **Acts 19:1–5**: And it came to pass, that while Apollos was at Corinth, Paul having passed through the upper coasts came to Ephesus: and finding certain disciples, *2* He said unto them, Have ye received the Holy Ghost since ye believed? And they said unto him, We have not so much as heard whether there be any Holy Ghost. *3* And he said unto them, Unto what then were ye baptized? And they said, Unto John's baptism. *4* Then said Paul, John verily baptized with the baptism of repentance, saying unto the people, that they should believe on Him which should come after him, that is, on Christ Jesus. *5* When they heard this, they were baptized in the name of the Lord Jesus. {*when learning new doctrine*}
7. **Acts 8:36–39:** And as they went on their way, they came unto a certain water: and the eunuch said, See, here is water; what doth hinder me to be baptized? *37* And Philip said, If thou believest with all thine heart thou mayest. And he answered and said, I believe that Jesus Christ is the Son of God. *38* And he commanded the chariot to stand still: and they went down both into the water, both Philip and the eunuch; and he baptized him. *39* And when they were come up out of the water, the Spirit of the Lord caught away Philip, that the eunuch saw him no more: and he went on his way rejoicing.
8. **Mark 1:9–11**: And it came to pass in those days, that Jesus came from Nazareth of Galilee, and was baptized of John in Jordan. *10* And straightway coming up out of the water, he saw the heavens opened,

and the Spirit like a dove descending upon Him. *11* And there came a voice from heaven, saying, Thou art my beloved Son, in whom I am well pleased.

9. **I Peter 2:21**: For even hereunto were ye called: because Christ also suffered for us, leaving us an example, that ye should follow His steps.
10. **John 3:22–23**: After these things came Jesus and His disciples into the land of Judea; and there He tarried with them, and baptized. *23* And John also was baptizing in AEnon near to Salim, because there was much water there: and they came, and were baptized. ... **John 4:2** (Though Jesus Himself baptized not, but His disciples.)
11. **Matthew 28:19–20**: Go ye therefore, and teach all nations, baptizing them in the name of the Father, and of the Son, and of the Holy Ghost: *20* Teaching them to observe all things whatsoever I have commanded you: and lo, I am with you alway, even unto the end of the world. Amen.

12—The Spirit of Prophecy

1. **Revelation 12:17**: And the dragon was wroth with the woman, and went to make war with the remnant of her seed, which keep the commandments of God, and have the testimony of Jesus Christ.
2. **Revelation 19:10**: And I fell at his feet to worship him. And he said unto me, See thou do it not: I am thy fellow servant, and of thy brethren that have the testimony of Jesus: worship God: for the testimony of Jesus is the spirit of prophecy.
3. **II Peter 1:19–21**: We have also a more sure word of prophecy; whereunto ye do well that ye take heed, as unto a light that shineth in a dark place, until the day dawn, and the day star arise in your hearts: *20* Knowing this first, that no prophecy of the scripture is of any private interpretation. *21* For the prophecy came not in old time by the will of man: but holy men of God spake as they were moved by the Holy Ghost.
4. **Amos 3:7**: Surely the Lord God will do nothing, but He revealeth His secret unto His servants the prophets.
5. **Matthew 7:15**: Beware of false prophets, which come to you in sheep's clothing, but inwardly they are ravening wolves. … **I John 4:1** Beloved, believe not every spirit, but try the spirits whether they are of God: because many false prophets are gone out into the world.
6. **Matthew 24:24**: For there shall arise false Christs, and false prophets and shall shew great signs and wonders; insomuch that, if it were possible, they shall deceive the very elect.
7. **Isaiah 8:20**: To the law and to the testimony: if they speak not according to this word, it is because there is no light in them.
8. **Matthew 7:20**: Wherefore by their fruits ye shall know them.
9. **Daniel 10:8–9, 17**: Therefore I was left alone, and saw this great vision, and there remained no strength in me: for my comeliness was turned in me into corruption, and I retained no strength. *9* Yet heard I the voice of His words: and when I heard the voice of His words, then was I in a deep sleep on my face, and my face toward the ground. … *17* For how can the servant of this my lord talk with this my lord? for as for me, straightway there remained no strength in me, neither is there breath left in me.

10. **Jeremiah 28:9:** The prophet which prophesieth of peace, when the word of the prophet shall come to pass, then shall the prophet be known, that the Lord hath truly sent him. *(see also Deuteronomy 18:22)*
11. **Ephesians 4:11–14**: And He gave some, apostles; and some, prophets; and some, evangelists; and some, pastors and teachers; *12* For the perfecting of the saints, for the work of the ministry, for the edifying of the body of Christ: *13* Till we all come in the unity of the faith, and of the knowledge of the Son of God, unto a perfect man, unto the measure of the stature of the fullness of Christ: *14* That we henceforth be no more children, tossed to and fro, and carried about with every wind of doctrine, by the sleight of men, and cunning craftiness, whereby they lie in wait to deceive.
12. **Acts 2:17**: And it shall come to pass in the last days, saith God, I will pour out of my Spirit upon all flesh: and your sons and your daughters shall prophesy, and your young men shall see visions, and your old men shall dream dreams. *(see also Joel 2:28–29)*

13—Healthful Living

1. **Genesis 1:29**: And God said, Behold, I have given you every herb bearing seed, which is upon the face of all the earth, and every tree, in the which is the fruit of a tree yielding seed; to you it shall be for meat. {*fruits, nuts, and grains*}
2. **Genesis 3:18**: Thorns also and thistles shall it bring forth to thee; and thou shalt eat the herb of the field. {*vegetables*}
3. **Genesis 9:3–4**: Every moving thing that liveth shall be meat for you; even as the green herb have I given you all things. *4* But flesh with the life thereof, which is the blood thereof, shall ye not eat. {*after the flood*}
4. **Genesis 7:2**: Of every clean beast thou shalt take to thee by sevens, the male and his female: and of beasts that are not clean by two, the male and his female.
5. **Deuteronomy 14:3, 6, 9**: Thou shalt not eat any abominable thing.... *6* And every beast that parteth the hoof, and cleaveth the cleft into two claws, and cheweth the cud among the beasts, that ye shall eat.... *9* These ye shall eat of all that are in the waters: all that have fins and scales shall ye eat. {*see also Lev. 11*}
6. **Proverbs 17:22**: A merry heart doeth good like a medicine: but a broken spirit drieth the bones.
7. **I Corinthians 10:31**: Whether therefore ye eat, or drink, or whatsoever ye do, do all to the glory of God.
8. **Proverbs 23:2–3**: And put a knife to thy throat, if thou be a man given to appetite. *3* Be not desirous of his dainties: for they are deceitful meat.
9. **Proverbs 23:31–32**: Look not thou upon the wine when it is red, when it giveth his color in the cup, when it moveth itself aright. *32* At the last it biteth like a serpent, and stingeth like an adder.... **Proverbs 20:21** Wine is a mocker, strong drink is raging: and whosoever is deceived thereby is not wise.
10. **I Corinthians 3:16–17**: Know ye not that ye are the temple of God, and that the Spirit of God dwelleth in you? *17* If any man defile the temple of God, him shall God destroy; for the temple of God is holy, which temple ye are. *(see also I Corinthians 6:19–20)*

11. **Romans 6:16**: Know ye not, that to whom ye yield yourselves servants to obey, his servants ye are to whom ye obey; whether of sin unto death, or of obedience unto righteousness?
12. **Romans 12:1–2**: I beseech you therefore, brethren, by the mercies of God, that ye present your bodies a living sacrifice, holy, acceptable unto God, which is your reasonable service. *2* And be not conformed to this world: but be ye transformed by the renewing of your mind, that ye may prove what is that good, and acceptable, and perfect, will of God.

14—Stewardship

1. **Matthew 6:31–33**: Therefore take no thought, saying, What shall we eat? or, What shall we drink? or, Wherewithal shall we be clothed? *32* (For after all these things do the Gentiles seek:) for your heavenly Father knoweth that ye have need of all these things. *33* But seek ye first the kingdom of God, and His righteousness; and all these things shall be added unto you.
2. **Psalm 24:1**: The earth is the Lord's, and the fullness thereof; the world, and they that dwell therein.
3. **Deuteronomy 8:18**: But thou shalt remember the Lord thy God: for it is He that giveth thee power to get wealth, that He may establish His covenant which He sware unto thy fathers, as it is this day.
4. **Matthew 6:19–21**: Lay not up for yourselves treasures upon earth, where moth and rust doth corrupt, and where thieves break through and steal: *20* But lay up for yourselves treasures in heaven, where neither moth nor rust doth corrupt, and where thieves do not break through nor steal: *21* For where your treasure is, there will your heart be also.
5. **Leviticus 27:32:** And concerning the tithe of the herd, or of the flock, even of whatsoever passeth under the rod, the tenth shall be holy unto the Lord.
6. **Malachi 3:8–11:** Will a man rob God? Yet ye have robbed Me. But ye say, Wherein have we robbed Thee? In tithes and offerings. *9* Ye are cursed with a curse: for ye have robbed Me, even this whole nation. *10* Bring ye all the tithes into the storehouse, that there may be meat in mine house, and prove me now herewith, saith the Lord of hosts, if I will not open you the windows of heaven, and pour you out a blessing, that there shall not be room enough to receive it. *11* And I will rebuke the devourer for your sakes, and he shall not destroy the fruits of your ground; neither shall your vine cast her fruit before the time in the field, saith the Lord of hosts.
7. **Numbers 18:21**: And behold, I have given the children of Levi all the tenth in Israel for an inheritance, for their service which they serve, even the service of the tabernacle of the congregation. {*the Levites were as the ministers of the temple*}
8. **I Corinthians 9:11–14**: If we have sown unto you spiritual things, is it a great thing if we shall reap your carnal things? *12* If others be partakers of this power over you, are not we rather? Nevertheless we

have not used this power; but suffer all things, lest we should hinder the gospel of Christ. *13* Do ye not know that they which minister about holy things live of the things of the temple? and they which wait at the altar are partakers with the altar? *14* Even so hath the Lord ordained that they which preach the gospel should live of the gospel. {*the tithe goes to pay the ministers*}

9. **Psalm 96:8**: Give unto the Lord the glory due unto His name: bring an offering, and come into His courts.
10. **Deuteronomy 16:17**: Every man shall give as he is able, according to the blessing of the Lord thy God which He hath given thee.
11. **II Corinthians 9:7**: Every man according as he purposeth in his heart, so let him give; not grudgingly, or of necessity: for God loveth a cheerful giver.

15—The Sanctuary

1. **Exodus 25:8**: And let them make Me a sanctuary; that I may dwell among them.
2. **Hebrews 9:2–5**: For there was a tabernacle made; the first, wherein was the candlestick, and the table, and the shewbread; which is called the sanctuary. *3* And after the second veil, the tabernacle which is called the Holiest of all; *4* Which had the golden censer, and the ark of the covenant overlaid round about with gold, wherein was the golden pot that had manna, and Aaron's rod that budded, and the tables of the covenant; *5* And over it the cherubims of glory shadowing the mercyseat; of which we cannot now speak particularly.
3. **Deuteronomy 10:4–5**: And he wrote on the tables, according to the first writing, the ten commandments, which the Lord spake unto you in the mount out of the midst of the fire in the day of the assembly: and the Lord gave them unto me. *5* And I turned myself and came down from the mount, and put the tables in the ark which I had made; and there they be, as the Lord commanded me.
4. **Leviticus 4:27–29**: And if any one of the common people sin through ignorance, while he doeth somewhat against any of the commandments of the Lord concerning things which ought not to be done, and be guilty; *28* Or if his sin, which he hath sinned, come to his knowledge: then he shall bring his offering, a kid of the goats, a female without blemish, for his sin which he hath sinned. *29* And he shall lay his hand upon the head of the sin offering, and slay the sin offering in the place of the burnt offering.
5. **Leviticus 16:8, 33–34**: And Aaron shall cast lots upon the two goats; one lot for the Lord, and the other lot for the scapegoat. …*33* And he shall make an atonement for the holy sanctuary, and he shall make an atonement for the tabernacle of the congregation, and for the altar, and he shall make an atonement for the priests, and for all the people of the congregation. *34* And this shall be an everlasting statute unto you, to make an atonement for the children of Israel for all their sins once a year. And he did as the Lord commanded Moses.
6. **John 1:29**: The next day John seeth Jesus coming unto him, and saith, Behold the Lamb of God, which taketh away the sin of the world.
7. **Hebrews 9:24**: For Christ is not entered into the holy places made with hands, which are the figures of the true; but into heaven itself, now to appear in the presence of God for us.

8. **Hebrews 8:2**: A minister of the sanctuary, and of the true tabernacle, which the Lord pitched, and not man.... **Hebrews 9:11** But Christ being come an high priest of good things to come, by a greater and more perfect tabernacle, not made with hands, that is to say, not of this building.
9. **Hebrews 9:22–23**: And almost all things are by the law purged with blood; and without shedding of blood is no remission. *23* It was therefore necessary that the patterns of things in the heavens should be purified with these; but the heavenly things themselves with better sacrifices than these.
10. **Daniel 8:14:** And he said unto me, Unto two thousand and three hundred days; then shall the sanctuary be cleansed. {*day = year in prophecy. From 457 BC (Ezra 7:11–28) to1844=2300*}
11. **Acts 4:12:** Neither is there salvation in any other: for there is none other name under heaven given among men, whereby we must be saved.

16—The Judgement

1. **Acts 17:30–31**: And the times of this ignorance God winked at; but now commandeth all men every where to repent: *31* Because He hath appointed a day, in the which He will judge the world in righteousness by that Man whom He hath ordained; whereof He hath given assurance unto all men, in that He hath raised Him from the dead. {*Jesus is our Judge and the judgment is going on in heaven now*}
2. **Ecclesiastes 3:17**: I said in mine heart, God shall judge the righteous and the wicked: for there is a time there for every purpose and for every work.
3. **Ecclesiastes 12:14**: For God shall bring every work into judgment, with every secret thing, whether it be good or whether it be evil.
4. **Revelation 20:12**: And I saw the dead, small and great, stand before God; and the books were opened: and another book was opened, which is the book of life: and the dead were judged out of those things which were written in the books, according to their works.
5. **Revelation 3:5**: He that overcometh, the same shall be clothed in white raiment; and I will not blot out his name out of the book of life, but I will confess his name before My Father, and before His angels.
6. **Matthew 25:31–41**: When the Son of man shall come in His glory, and all the holy angels with Him, then shall He sit upon the throne of His glory: *32* And before Him shall be gathered all nations: and He shall separate them one from another, as a shepherd divideth his sheep from the goats: *33* And He shall set the sheep on His right hand, but the goats on the left. *34* Then shall the King say unto them on His right hand, Come, ye blessed of My Father, inherit the kingdom prepared for you from the foundation of the world: *35* For I was an hungered, and ye gave Me meat: I was thirsty, and ye gave Me drink: I was a stranger, and ye took Me in: *36* Naked, and ye clothed Me: I was sick, and ye visited Me: I was in prison, and ye came unto Me. *37* Then shall the righteous answer Him, saying, Lord, when saw we Thee an hungered, and fed Thee? or thirsty, and gave Thee drink? *38* When saw we Thee a stranger, and took Thee in? or naked, and clothed Thee? *39* Or when saw we Thee sick, or in prison, and came unto Thee? *40* And the King shall answer and say unto them, Verily I say unto you, Inasmuch as ye have done it unto one of the least of these my brethren, ye have done it unto Me. *41* Then shall He say also unto them on

the left hand, Depart from Me, ye cursed, into everlasting fire, prepared for the devil and his angels.

7. **II Corinthians 5:10**: For we must all appear before the judgment seat of Christ; that everyone may receive the things done in his body, according to that he hath done, whether it be good or bad.
8. **Romans 14:12**: So then every one of us shall give account of himself to God.
9. **I Corinthians 6:2–3**: Do ye not know that the saints shall judge the world? and if the world shall be judged by you, are ye unworthy to judge the smallest matters? *3* Know ye not that we shall judge angels? how much more things that pertain to this life? {*see also Dan. 7:22*}
10. **I Peter 4:17:** For the time is come that judgment must begin at the house of God: and if it first begin at us, what shall the end be of them that obey not the gospel of God?
11. **Revelation 22:12**: And, behold, I come quickly; and my reward is with Me, to give every man according as his work shall be.

17—Church Standards

1. **Philippians 4:8**: Finally, brethren, whatsoever things are true, whatsoever things are honest, whatsoever things are just, whatsoever things are pure, whatsoever things are lovely, whatsoever things are of good report; if there be any virtue, and if there be any praise, think on these things.
2. **I Corinthians 10:31**: Whether therefore ye eat, or drink, or whatsoever ye do, do all to the glory of God.
3. **Ephesians 4:29–32**: Let no corrupt communication proceed out of your mouth, but that which is good to the use of edifying, that it may minister grace unto the hearers. *30* And grieve not the holy Spirit of God, whereby ye are sealed unto the day of redemption. *31* Let all bitterness, and wrath, and anger, and clamour, and evil speaking, be put away from you, with all malice: *32* And be ye kind one to another, tenderhearted, forgiving one another, even as God for Christ's sake hath forgiven you.
4. **Ephesians 5:3–4**: But fornication, and all uncleanness, or covetousness, let it not be once named among you, as becometh saints; *4* Neither filthiness, nor foolish talking, nor jesting, which are not convenient: but rather giving of thanks.
5. **Ephesians 5:22, 25**: Wives, submit yourselves unto your own husbands, as unto the Lord….*25* Husbands, love your wives, even as Christ also loved the church, and gave Himself for it.
6. **I Corinthians 7:10**: And unto the married I command, yet not I, but the Lord, Let not the wife depart from her husband.
7. **Romans 12:1–2:** I beseech you therefore, brethren, by the mercies of God, that ye present your bodies a living sacrifice, holy, acceptable unto God, which is your reasonable service. *2* And be not conformed to this world: but be ye transformed by the renewing of your mind, that ye may prove what is that good, and acceptable, and perfect will of God.
8. **I Peter 3:3–4**: Whose adorning let it not be that outward adorning of plaiting the hair, and of wearing of gold, or of putting on of apparel: *4* But let it be the hidden man of the heart, in that which is not corruptible, even the ornament of a meek and quiet spirit, which is in the sight of God of great price. *(see also I Timothy 2:9–10)*

9. **Revelation 17:4–5**: And the woman was arrayed in purple and scarlet colour, and decked with gold and precious stones and pearls, having a golden cup in her hand full of abominations and filthiness of her fornication: *5* And upon her forehead was a name written, MYSTERY, BABYLON THE GREAT, THE MOTHER OF HARLOTS AND ABOMINATIONS OF THE EARTH.
10. **Revelation 12:1**: And There appeared a great wonder in heaven; a woman clothed with the sun, and the moon under her feet, and upon her head a crown of twelve stars:
11. **II Peter 3:13–14**: Nevertheless we, according to His promise, look for new heavens and a new earth, wherein dwelleth righteousness. *14* Wherefore, beloved, seeing that ye look for such things, be diligent that ye may be found of Him in peace, without spot, and blameless.

18—State of the Dead

1. **Genesis 2:17**: But of the tree of the knowledge of good and evil, thou shalt not eat of it: for in the day that thou eatest thereof thou shalt surely die.
2. **Genesis 3:1–4**: Now the serpent was more subtil than any beast of the field which the Lord God had made. And he said unto the woman, Yea, hath God said, Ye shall not eat of every tree of the garden? *2* And the woman said unto the serpent, We may eat of the fruit of the trees of the garden: *3* But of the fruit of the tree which is in the midst of the garden, God hath said, Ye shall not eat of it, neither shall ye touch it, lest ye die. *4* And the serpent said unto the woman, Ye shall not surely die.
3. **I Timothy 6:14–16**: That thou keep this commandment without spot, unrebukeable, until the appearing of our Lord Jesus Christ: *15* Which in His times He shall shew, who is the blessed and only Potentate, the King of kings, and Lord of lords; *16* Who only hath immortality, dwelling in the light which no man can approach unto; whom no man hath seen, nor can see: to Whom be honour and power everlasting. Amen.
4. **Ezekiel 18:4:** Behold, all souls are mine; as the soul of the father, so also the soul of the son is mine: the soul that sinneth, it shall die.
5. **Ecclesiastes 9:5**: For the living know that they shall die: but the dead know not any thing, neither have they any more a reward; for the memory of them is forgotten.
6. **Psalm 146:4**: His breath goeth forth, he returneth to his earth; in that very day his thoughts perish.
7. **John 11:11–14**: These things said He: and after that He saith unto them, Our friend Lazarus sleepeth; but I go, that I may awake him out of sleep. 12 Then said His disciples, Lord, if he sleep, he shall do well. 13 Howbeit Jesus spake of his death: but they thought that He had spoken of taking of rest in sleep. 14 Then said Jesus unto them plainly. Lazarus is dead.
8. **Ecclesiastes 12:7**: Then shall the dust return to the earth as it was: and the spirit shall return unto God who gave it.
9. **Job 27:3**: All the while my breath is in me, and the spirit of God is in my nostrils.
10. **Genesis 2:7**: And the Lord God formed man of the dust of the ground, and breathed into his nostrils the breath of life; and man became a living soul. {*Dust + Breath = Living Soul*}

11. **John 5:28–29**: Marvel not at this: for the hour is coming, in the which all that are in the graves shall hear His voice, *29* And shall come forth; they that have done good, unto the resurrection of life; and they that have done evil, unto the resurrection of damnation.
12. **I Thessalonians 4:16–17**: For the Lord Himself shall descend from heaven with a shout, with the voice of the archangel, and with the trump of God: and the dead in Christ shall rise first: *17* Then we which are alive and remain shall be caught up together with them in the clouds, to meet the Lord in the air: and so shall we ever be with the Lord. {*Christ's second coming*}
13. **I Corinthians 15:51–55**: Behold, I shew you a mystery; We shall not all sleep, but we shall all be changed, *52* In a moment, in the twinkling of an eye, at the last trump: for the trumpet shall sound, and the dead shall be raised incorruptible, and we shall be changed. *53* For this corruptible must put on incorruption, and this mortal must put on immortality. *54* So when this corruptible shall have put on incorruption, and this mortal shall have put on immortality, then shall be brought to pass the saying that is written, Death is swallowed up in victory. *55* O death, where is thy sting? O grave, where is thy victory?

19—The Millennium

1. **Revelation 6:14–17**: And the heaven departed as a scroll when it is rolled together; and every mountain and island were moved out of their places. *15* And the kings of the earth, and the great men, and the rich men, and the chief captains, and the mighty men, and every bondman, and every free man, hidthemselves in the dens and in the rocks of the mountains; *16* And said to the mountains and rocks, Fall on us, and hide us from the face of Him that sitteth on the throne, and from the wrath of the Lamb: *17* For the great day of His wrath is come; and who shall be able to stand?
2. **II Thessalonians 1:7–9**: And to you who are troubled rest with us, when the Lord Jesus shall be revealed from heaven with His mighty angels, *8* In flaming fire taking vengeance on them that know not God, and that obey not the gospel of our Lord Jesus Christ: *9* Who shall be punished with everlasting destruction from the presence of the Lord, and from the glory of His power.
3. **Revelation 20:1–3**: And I saw an angel come down from heaven, having the key of the bottomless pit and a great chain in his hand. *2* And he laid hold on the dragon, that old serpent, which is the Devil, and Satan, and bound him a thousand years, *3* And cast him into the bottomless pit, and shut him up, and set a seal upon him, that he should deceive the nations no more, till the thousand years should be fulfilled: and after that he must be loosed a little season.
4. **Revelation 20:5–6**: But the rest of the dead lived not again until the thousand years were finished. This is the first resurrection. *6* Blessed and holy is he that hath part in the first resurrection: on such the second death hath no power, but they shall be priests of God and of Christ, and shall reign with Him a thousand years.
5. **Revelation 20:14–15**: And death and hell were cast into the lake of fire. This is the second death. *15* And whosoever was not found written in the book of life was cast into the lake of fire. (*see also Revelation 21:8*)
6. **Revelation 20:4**: And I saw thrones, and they sat upon them, and judgment was given unto them: and I saw the souls of them that were beheaded for the witness of Jesus, and for the word of God, and which had not worshipped the beast, neither his image, neither had received

his mark upon their foreheads, or in their hands; and they lived and reigned with Christ a thousand years. *(see also I Corinthians 6:2–3)*

7. **Jeremiah 4:23–26**: I beheld the earth, and, lo, it was without form, and void; and the heavens, and they had no light. *24* I beheld the mountains, and, lo, they trembled, and all the hills moved lightly. *25* I beheld, and, lo, there was no man, and all the birds of the heavens were fled. *26* I beheld, and, lo, the fuitful place was a wilderness, and all the cities thereof were broken down at the presence of the Lord, and by His fierce anger.
8. **Revelation 20:7–10**: And when the thousand years are expired, Satan shall be loosed out of his prison, *8* And shall go out to deceive the nations which are in the four quarters of the earth, Gog and Magog, to gather them together to battle: the number of whom is as the sand of the sea. *9* And they went up on the breadth of the earth, and compassed the camp of the saints about, and the beloved city: and fire came down from God out of heaven, and devoured them, *10* And the devil that deceived them was cast into the lake of fire and brimstone, where the beast and the false prophet are and shall be tormented day and night for ever and ever.
9. **Revelation 21:3–4**: And I heard a great voice out of heaven saying, Behold, the tabernacle of God is with men, and He will dwell with them, and they shall be His people, and God Himself shall be with them, and be their God. *4* And God shall wipe away all tears from their eyes; and there shall be no more death, neither sorrow, nor crying, neither shall there be any more pain: for the former things are passed away.

20—The Little Horn

1. **Daniel 7:4–7**: *First beast*—The first was like a lion, and had eagle's wings. I beheld til the wings thereof were plucked, and it was lifted up from the earth, and made stand upon the feet as a man, and a man's heart was given to it. *5 Second beast*—And behold another beast, a second, like to a bear, and it raised itself up on one side, and it had three ribs in the mouth of it between the teeth of it: and they said thus unto it, Arise, devour much flesh. *6 Third beast*—After this I beheld, and lo another, like a leopard, which had upon the back of it four wings of a fowl; the beast had also four heads; and dominion was given to it. *7 Fourth beast*—After this I saw in the night visions, and behold a fourth beast, dreadful and terrible, and strong exceedingly; and it had great iron teeth: it devoured and brake in pieces, and stamped the residue with the feet of it: and it was diverse from all the beasts that were before it; and it had ten horns.
2. **Daniel 7:17:** These great beasts, which are four, are four kings, which shall arise out of the earth. {*kings or kingdoms*}
3. **Daniel 7:8**: I considered the horns, and, behold, there came up among them another little horn, before whom there were three of the first horns plucked up by the roots: and, behold, in this horn were eyes like the eyes of man, and a mouth speaking great things.
4. **Mark 2:7**: Why doth this man thus speak blasphemies? who can forgive sins but God only?
5. **John 10:33**: The Jews answered Him, saying, For a good work we stone Thee not; but for blasphemy; and because that Thou, being a man, makest Thyself God.
6. **Daniel 7:20–21**: And of the ten horns that were in his head, and of the other which came up, and before whom three fell; even of that horn that had eyes, and a mouth that spake very great things, whose look was more stout than his fellows. *21* I beheld, and the same horn made war with the saints, and prevailed against them.
7. **Daniel 7:25**: And he shall speak great words against the most High, and shall wear out the saints of the most High, and think to change times and laws: and they shall be given into his hand until a time and times and the dividing of time.

8. **Acts 20:29–30**: For I know this, that after my departing shall grievous wolves enter in among you, not sparing the flock. *30* Also of your own selves shall men arise, speaking perverse things, to draw away disciples after them.
9. **II Thessalonians 2:3–4:** Let no man deceive you by any means: for that day shall not come, except there come a falling away first, and that man of sin be revealed, the son of perdition; *4* Who opposeth and exalteth himself above all that is called God, or that is worshipped; so that he as God sitteth in the temple of God, shewing himself that he is God.
10. **Daniel 7:27**: And the kingdom and dominion, and the greatness of the kingdom under the whole heaven, shall be given to the people of the saints of the most High, whose kingdom is an everlasting kingdom, and all dominions shall serve and obey Him.

21—Mark of the Beast

1. **Exodus 20:8–11**: Remember the Sabbath day to keep it holy. *9* Six days shalt thou labour, and do all thy work: *10* But the seventh day is the Sabbath of the Lord thy God: in it thou shalt not do any work, thou, nor thy son, nor thy daughter, thy manservant, nor thy maidservant, nor thy cattle, nor thy stranger that is within thy gates: *11* For in six days the Lord made heaven and earth, the sea, and all that in them is, and rested the seventh day: wherefore the Lord blessed the Sabbath day, and hallowed it. {*Seal contains: Name [Lord], Title [creator], and Territory [heaven, earth, and sea]*}
2. **Exodus 31:16–17**: Wherefore the children of Israel shall keep the Sabbath, to observe the Sabbath throughout their generations, for a perpetual covenant. *17* It is a sign between Me and the children of Israel for ever: for in six days the Lord made heaven and earth, and on the seventh day He rested, and was refreshed.
3. **Galatians 3:26–29**: For ye are all the children of God by faith in Christ Jesus. *27* For as many of you as have been baptized into Christ have put on Christ. *28* There is neither Jew nor Greek, there is neither bond nor free, there is neither male nor female: for ye are all one in Christ Jesus. *29* And if ye be Christ's, then are ye Abraham's seed, and heirs according to the promise.
4. **Revelation 7:2–3**: And I saw another angel ascending from the east, having the seal of the living God: and he cried with a loud voice to the four angels, to whom it was given to hurt the earth and the sea, *3* Saying, Hurt not the earth, neither the sea, nor the trees, till we have sealed the servants of our God in their foreheads.
5. **Revelation 7:4:** And I heard the number of them which were sealed: and there were sealed an hundred and forty and four thousand of all the tribes of the children of Israel. *(see verse 14)*
6. **Revelation 12:17**: And the dragon was wroth with the woman, and went to make war with the remnant of her seed, which keep the commandments of God, and have the testimony of Jesus Christ.
7. **Revelation 13:1–3**: And I stood upon the sand of the sea, and saw a beast rise up out of the sea, having seven heads and ten horns, and upon his horns ten crowns, and upon this heads the name of blasphemy. *2* And the beast which I saw was like unto a leopard, and his feet were as the feet of a bear, and his mouth as the mouth of a lion:

and the dragon gave him his power, and his seat, and great authority. *3* And I saw one of his heads as it were wounded to death; and his deadly wound was healed: and all the world wondered after the beast. *(see also verses 4–8)*

8. **II Thessalonians 2:3–4**: Let no man deceive you by any means: for that day shall not come, except there come a falling away first, and that man of sin be revealed, the son of perdition; *4* Who opposeth and exalteth himself above all that is called God, or that is worshipped; so that he as God sitteth in the temple of God, shewing himself that he is God. {*the papacy*}
9. **Revelation 13:15–18**: And he had power to give life unto the image of the beast, that the image of the beast should both speak, and cause that as many as would not worship the image of the beast should be killed. *16* And he causeth all, both small and great, rich and poor, free and bond, to receive a mark in their right hand, or in their foreheads: *17* And that no man might buy or sell, save he that had the mark, or the name of the beast, or the number of his name. *18* Here is wisdom. Let him that hath understanding count the number of the beast: for it is the number of a man; and his number is Six hundred threescore and six. {*VICARIUS: 5+1+100+1+5; FILII: 1+50+1+1; DEI: 500+1 = 666*}
10. **Revelation 20:10**: And the devil that deceived them was cast into the lake of fire and brimstone, where the beast and the false prophet are, and shall be tormented day and night for ever and ever.

22—Three Angels' Messages

1. **Revelation 14:6–7**: And I saw another angel fly in the midst of heaven, having the everlasting gospel to preach unto them that dwell on the earth, and to every nation, and kindred, and tongue, and people, *7* Saying with a loud voice, Fear God, and give glory to Him; for the hour of His judgment is come: and worship Him that made heaven, and earth, and the sea, and the fountains of waters.
2. **Exodus 31:16–17**: Wherefore the children of Israel shall keep the Sabbath, to observe the Sabbath throughout their generations, for a perpetual covenant. *17* It is a sign between Me and the children of Israel for ever: for in six days the Lord made heaven and earth, and on the seventh day He rested, and was refreshed.
3. **Revelation 14:8**: And there followed another angel, saying, Babylon is fallen, is fallen, that great city, because she made all nations drink of the wine of the wrath of her fornication.
4. **Revelation 13:3–5:** And I saw one of his heads as it were wounded to death; and his deadly wound was healed: and all the world wondered after the beast. *4* And they worshipped the dragon which gave power unto the beast: and they worshipped the beast, saying, Who is like unto the beast? who is able to make war with him? *5* And there was given unto him a mouth speaking great things and blasphemies; and power was given unto him to continue forty and two months.... **Revelation 16:13–14**: And I saw three unclean spirits like frogs come out of the mouth of the dragon, and out of the mouth of the beast, and out of the mouth of the false prophet. *14* For they are the spirits of devils, working miracles, which go forth unto the kings of the earth and of the whole world, to gather them to the battle of that great day of God Almighty. *(see also Revelation 17:8–9)*
5. **Revelation 18:2**: And he cried mightily with a strong voice, saying, Babylon the great is fallen, is fallen, and is become the habitation of devils, and the hold of every foul spirit, and a cage of every unclean and hateful bird.
6. **Revelation 14:9–11**: And the third angel followed them, saying with a loud voice, If any man worship the beast and his image, and receive his mark in his forehead, or in his hand, *10* The same shall drink of the wine of the wrath of God, which is poured out without mixture into the cup of his indignation; and he shall be tormented with fire and

brimstone in the presence of the holy angels, and in the presence of the Lamb: *11* And the smoke of their torment ascendeth up for ever and ever: and they have no rest day nor night, who worship the beast and his image, and whosoever receiveth the mark of his name.

7. **Revelation 13:11–12**: And I beheld another beast coming up out of the earth; and he had two horns like a lamb, and he spake as a dragon {*USA*}. *12* And he exerciseth all the power of the first beast before him, and causeth the earth and them which dwell therein to worship the first beast, whose deadly wound was healed.
8. **Revelation 13:15–18:** And he had power to give life unto the image of the beast, that the image of the beast should both speak, and cause that as many as would not worship the image of the beast should be killed. *16* And he causeth all, both small and great, rich and poor, free and bond to receive a mark in their right hand, or in their foreheads: *17* And that no man might buy or sell, save he that had the mark, or the name of the beast, or the number of his name. *18* Here is wisdom. Let him that hath understanding count the number of the beast: for it is the number of a man; and his number is Six hundred threescore and six.
9. **Revelation 14:12:** Here is the patience of the saints: here are they that keep the commandments of God, and the faith of Jesus.
10. **Revelation 15:2**: And I saw as it were a sea of glass mingled with fire: and them that had gotten the victory over the beast, and over his image, and over his mark, and over the number of his name, stand on the sea of glass, having the harps of God.

23—Seven Last Plagues

1. **Revelation 16:1–2**: And I heard a great voice out of the temple saying to the seven angels, Go your ways, and pour out the vials of the wrath of God upon the earth. *2* And the first went, and poured out his vial upon the earth; and there fell a noisome and grievous sore upon the men which had the mark of the beast, and upon them which worshipped his image.
2. **Revelation 16:3**: And the second angel poured out his vial upon the sea; and it became as the blood of a dead man: and every living soul died in the sea.
3. **Revelation 16:4**: And the third angel poured out his vial upon the rivers and fountains of waters; and they became blood.
4. **Revelation 16:5–6**: And I heard the angel of the waters say, Thou art righteous, O Lord, which art, and wast, and shalt be, because Thou hast judged thus. *6* For they have shed the blood of saints and prophets, and Thou hast given them blood to drink; for they are worthy.
5. **Revelation 16:8**: And the fourth angel poured out his vial upon the sun; and power was given unto him to scorch men with fire.
6. **Revelation 16:10**: And the fifth angel poured out his vial upon the seat of the beast; and his kingdom was full of darkness; and they gnawed their tongues for pain.
7. **Revelation 16:12**: And the sixth angel poured out his vial upon the great river Euphrates; and the water thereof was dried up, that the way of the kings of the east might be prepared.
8. **Revelation 16:17–21**: And the seventh angel poured out his vial into the air; and there came a great voice out of the temple of heaven, from the throne, saying, It is done. *18* And there were voices, and thunders, and lightnings; and there was a great earthquake, such as was not since men were upon the earth, so mighty an earthquake, and so great. *19* And the great city was divided into three parts, and the cities of the nations fell: and great Babylon came in remembrance before God, to give unto her the cup of the wine of the fierceness of His wrath. *20* And every island fled away, and the mountains were not found. *21* And there fell upon men a great hail out of heaven, every stone about the weight of a talent: and men blasphemed God because of the plague of the hail; for the plague thereof was exceeding great.

9. **Revelation 17:1, 3–6:** And there came one of the seven angels which had the seven vials, and talked with me, saying unto me, Come hither; I will shew unto thee the judgment of the great whore that sitteth upon many waters: ... 3 So he carried me away in the spirit into the wilderness: and I saw a woman sit upon a scarlet coloured beast, full of names of blasphemy, having seven heads and ten horns. 4 And the woman was arrayed in purple and scarlet colour, and decked with gold and precious stones and pearls, having a golden cup in her hand full of abominations and filthiness of her fornication: 5 And upon her forehead was a name written, MYSTERY, BABYLON THE GREAT, THE MOTHER OF HARLOTS AND ABOMINATIONS OF THE EARTH. 6 And I saw the woman drunken with the blood of the saints, and with the blood of the martyrs of Jesus: and when I saw her, I wondered with great admiration. *(see also Revelation 18:2, 8)*
10. **Revelation 18:4:** And I heard another voice from heaven, saying, Come out of her, my people, that ye be not partakers of her sins, and that ye receive not of her plagues.

24—Trust and Obey

1. **Psalm 139:23–24**: Search me, O God, and know my heart: try me, and know my thoughts; *24* And see if there be any wicked way in me, and lead me in the way everlasting.
2. **Luke 12:7**: But even the very hairs of your head are all numbered. Fear not therefore: ye are of more value than many sparrows.
3. **II Timothy 2:15**: Study to shew thyself approved unto God, a workman that needeth not to be ashamed, rightly dividing the word of truth. *(see also Ephesians 6:11)*
4. **Matthew 6:33**: But seek ye first the kingdom of God, and His righteousness; and all these things shall be added unto you.
5. **Matthew 7:7–8**: Ask, and it shall be given you; seek, and ye shall find; knock, and it shall be opened unto you: *8* For every one that asketh receiveth; and he that seeketh findeth; and to him that knocketh it shall be opened.
6. **John 14:14, 23**: If ye shall ask any thing in My name, I will do it....*23* Jesus answered and said unto him, If a man love Me, he will keep My words: and My Father will love him, and We will come unto him, and make Our abode with him.
7. **I John 5:1–4:** Whosoever believeth that Jesus is the Christ is born of God: and every one that loveth him that begat loveth him also that is begotten of him. *2* By this we know that we love the children of God, when we love God, and keep His commandments. *3* For this is the love of God, that we keep His commandments: and His commandments are not grievous. *4* For whatsoever is born of God overcometh the world: and this is the victory that overcometh the world, even our faith.
8. **James 4:17:** Therefore to him that knoweth to do good, and doeth it not, to him it is sin.
9. **Philippians 4:13**: I can do all things through Christ which strengtheneth me.
10. **James 4:7**: Submit yourselves therefore to God. Resist the devil, and he will flee from you.
11. **Revelation 22:14:** Blessed are they that do His commandments, that they may have right to the tree of life, and may enter in through the gates into the city.

25—The True Church

1. **Jeremiah 6:2**: I have likened the daughter of Zion to a comely and delicate woman. {*Woman = Church*}
2. **Revelation 12:1–2**: And there appeared a great wonder in heaven; a woman clothed with the sun, and the moon under her feet, and upon her head a crown of twelve stars: *2* And she being with child cried, travailing in birth, and pained to be delivered.
3. **Revelation 17:3–6**: So he carried me away in the spirit into the wilderness: and I saw a woman sit upon a scarlet coloured beast, full of names of blasphemy, having seven heads and ten horns. *4* And the woman was arrayed in purple and scarlet colour, and decked with gold and precious stones and pearls, having a golden cup in her hand full of abominations and filthiness of her fornication: *5* And upon her forehead was a name written, MYSTERY, BABYLON THE GREAT, THE MOTHER OF HARLOTS AND ABOMINATIONS OF THE EARTH. *6* And I saw the woman drunken with the blood of the saints, and with the blood of the martyrs of Jesus: and when I saw her, I wondered with great admiration.
4. **Revelation 12:6, 14**: And the woman fled into the wilderness, where she hath a place prepared of God, that they should feed her there a thousand two hundred and threescore days {*1260 days or years*}.... *14* And to the woman were given two wings of a great eagle, that she might fly into the wilderness, into her place, where she is nourished for a time, and times, and half a time, from the face of the serpent. {*Time = 1 year or 360 days; Times = 2 years or 720 days; Half time = 1/2 year or 180 days totaling 1260 days; or prophetic time, 1260 years*}
5. **Revelation 12:5:** And she brought forth a man child, who was to rule all nations with a rod of iron: and her child was caught up unto God, and to His throne. {*Jesus; see also Acts 1:9–1*}
6. **Revelation 14:12**: Here is the patience of the saints: here are they that keep the commandments of God, and the faith of Jesus.
7. **Revelation 12:17**: And the dragon was wroth with the woman, and went to make war with the remnant of her seed, which keep the commandments of God, and have the testimony of Jesus Christ.
8. **Revelation 19:10:** And I fell at his feet to worship him. And he said unto me, See thou do it not: I am thy fellow-servant, and of thy brethren

that have the testimony of Jesus: worship God: for the testimony of Jesus is the Spirit of prophecy.

9. **Jeremiah 23:1–4**: Woe be unto the pastors that destroy and scatter the sheep of my pasture! saith the Lord. *2* Therefore thus saith the Lord God of Israel against the pastors that feed my people; Ye have scattered my flock, and driven them away, and have not visited them: behold, I will visit upon you the evil of your doings, saith the Lord. *3* And I will gather the remnant of my flock out of all countries whither I have driven them, and will bring them again to their folds; and they shall be fruitful and increase. *4* And I will set up shepherds over them which shall feed them: and they shall fear no more, nor be dismayed, neither shall they be lacking, saith the Lord.
10. **Revelation 18:4**: And I heard another voice from heaven, saying, Come out of her, My people, that ye be not partakers of her sins, and that ye receive not of her plagues.

Find Peace, Power, and Purpose for Your Life!
amazingfacts.org
Enroll in our FREE online Bible study course and discover:
• What happens after death
• The way to better health
• How to save your marriage
• The surprising news about hell
• Why the Bible is relevant today
• The "mark of the beast"
• Who really gets "left behind"
• ... and much more!
Is There Anything Left You Can Trust?
Saved from Certain Death
Who Is the Antichrist?
Amazing Facts Study Guide 3
Are the Dead Really Dead?
Amazing Facts Study Guide 10
The USA in Bible Prophecy
Amazing Facts Study Guide 21
Or enroll in the postal mail course! Send your name and address to:
AMAZING FACTS
P.O. Box 909
Roseville, CA 95678
27 full-color, illustrated, Scripture-packed, easy-to-understand lessons!

www.ingramcontent.com/pod-product-compliance
Lightning Source LLC
Chambersburg PA
CBHW040316170426
43196CB00020B/2939
* 9 7 8 1 4 7 9 6 1 4 4 1 7 *